A TEACHER'S GUIDE FOR

Getting Serious

ABOUT THE

System

A TEACHER'S GUIDE FOR

Getting Serious

ABOUT THE

System

D'Ette Cowan
Stacey Joyner
Shirley Beckwith

CORWIN
A SAGE Company

CORWIN
A SAGE Company

FOR INFORMATION:

Corwin
A SAGE Company
2455 Teller Road
Thousand Oaks, California 91320
www.corwin.com

SAGE Publications Ltd.
1 Oliver's Yard
55 City Road
London, EC1Y 1SP
United Kingdom

SAGE Publications India Pvt. Ltd.
B 1/I 1 Mohan Cooperative Industrial Area
Mathura Road, New Delhi 110 044
India

SAGE Publications Asia-Pacific Pte. Ltd.
3 Church Street
#10-04 Samsung Hub
Singapore 049483

Acquisitions Editor: Arnis Burvikovs
Associate Editor: Joanna Coelho
Editorial Assistant: Kimberly Greenberg
Production Editor: Amy Schroller
Copy Editor: Brenda Weight
Typesetter: Hurix Systems Pvt. Ltd.
Proofreader: Victoria Reed-Castro
Cover Designer: Scott Van Atta
Permissions Editor: Karen Ehrmann

Copyright © 2012 by Corwin

A catalog record of this book is available from the Library of Congress.

ISBN 978-1-4522-0512-0

12 13 14 15 16 10 9 8 7 6 5 4 3 2 1

Contents

Publisher's Acknowledgments

Corwin would like to thank the following individuals for taking the time to provide their editorial insight and guidance:

Sally Bennett, Curriculum Coordinator
East Poinsett County School District
Lepanto, AR

Freda Hicks, Assistant Principal
Grady Brown Elementary School
Hillsborough, NC

Debbie Langford, Counselor
West Hills Elementary School
Bremerton School District
Bremerton, WA

Marianne Lescher, Principal
Kyrene de la Mariposa School
Gilbert, AZ

Luule Moreno, Independent Educational Consultant
McAllen, TX

Debra Paradowski, Associate Principal
Arrowhead Union High School
Hartland, WI

Diana Pratt, Assistant Principal
Kent Meridian High School
Kent, WA

Cynthia Stone, Director of School Improvement
South San Antonio ISD
San Antonio, TX

Kelly VanLaeken, Principal
Ruben A. Cirillo High School
Macedon, NY

About the Authors

D'Ette Cowan, EdD. Before retiring from SEDL in October 2010, Dr. Cowan led Texas Comprehensive Center efforts to assist state and intermediate agencies in providing high-needs districts and schools with technical assistance that is systemic in nature. In her 12-year career at SEDL, she also assisted low-performing districts and schools throughout a five-state region to improve student learning, and investigated strategies for transforming schools into professional learning communities. Currently, Dr. Cowan serves as a consultant to SEDL on a variety of projects.

As one of the researchers and authors of *Working Systemically in Action: A Guide for Facilitators*, Dr. Cowan has had first-hand experience in helping district and school leaders apply a systemic approach to improve learning outcomes for students. Her study of professional learning communities over her career has included conducting and applying research and presenting findings at conferences and in books and journals. She has authored chapters and articles in *Demystifying Professional Learning Communities: School Leadership at Its Best*; *SEDL Letter*; *Journal of School Leadership*; *Reculturing Schools as Professional Learning Communities*; and *Learning Together, Leading Together*.

Prior to joining SEDL in December 1997, Dr. Cowan served as a junior high school teacher and an elementary school principal. Her continuing research interests include leadership for change, systemic improvement, and professional learning communities.

Stacey Joyner is a Program Associate at SEDL. She participates in efforts to build state education staff capacity to serve districts and schools. She is the former editor of the USDE's Reading First newsletter *The Notebook*, and former editor of the Texas Comprehensive Center's newsletter *Texas Focus*. She is coauthor of SEDL's *Working Systemically in Action: A Guide for Facilitators* that describes a comprehensive process for district and school improvement.

Prior to joining SEDL, Ms. Joyner served as the Reading Coordinator for the Idaho State Department of Education. She has 11 years of teaching experience. She has served as a reading specialist and teacher trainer for the Clark County School District in Las Vegas, Nevada.

Ms. Joyner holds a BA in Elementary Education from Idaho State University and an MEd in Curriculum and Instruction from the University of Nevada at Las Vegas. She is currently a doctoral student at the University of Texas at Austin.

Shirley Beckwith is a Communications Associate with SEDL's Texas Comprehensive Center (TXCC). She provides editorial review of training materials and resources used in meetings hosted by the TXCC and prepares materials for submission to national evaluators. She also provides and reviews content for the TXCC website. She has been involved in several publications about the Working Systemically approach, including the 2008 *Working Systemically in Action: A Guide for Facilitators* and helped convert the process into a scripted training manual for school support teams.

Prior to joining SEDL, Ms. Beckwith worked for several years at the University of Texas LBJ School of Public Affairs as the coordinator and researcher for the *Guide to Texas State Agencies*. Ms. Beckwith has a master's degree in Library and Information Science.

Introduction to Systemic Improvement

SYSTEMS THINKING

Most of us can recall learning about icebergs at some point in our elementary school science classes. Perhaps the most fascinating fact we remember is that approximately 90% of an iceberg's mass lies below the surface of the water, with only a small portion of the iceberg visible above the surface. Thus, the expression "tip of the iceberg" often refers to how a problem manifests itself at a superficial level. The real causes for the problem lie deep below the surface.

One might ask, "What do icebergs have to do with systemic change?" Senge et al. (2000) use an iceberg analogy to illustrate the necessity of looking below surface events in order to truly understand and then solve school problems. Rather than addressing only the visible aspects of a problem, Senge et al. suggest probing deeper to identify *trends and patterns* in the behavior of an organization (e.g., a school system) to begin revealing the actual source of the problem. However, while identification of these trends and patterns over time is important in analyzing problems, Senge cautions that this information is still inadequate to understand and then address the underlying cause of the problem.

For deeper understanding, Senge and his colleagues suggest delving into *systemic structures* to reveal underlying forces (and interactions among these forces) that contribute to the trends and patterns in organizational behavior. By exploring this deeper level, one can discover fundamental aspects of the system that allow the problem to continue.

Yet, Senge et al. (2000) advocate looking even deeper to consider *mental models* existing within the organization that perpetuate undesirable systemic structures. Such mental models, which are shaped by the values, beliefs, and attitudes of those within the organization, influence both individual and collective views of how the district or school should work. Senge and colleagues propose that systemic thinkers go beyond merely recognizing such models and, instead, honestly question their validity. Challenging these mental models often helps get to the underlying cause of the problem and set the organization on the path toward systemic change.

1

Systems Thinking in Education

What, then, does systemic thinking have to do with district and school improvement? In 2004, Dennis Sparks, former executive director of the National Staff Development Council (now Learning Forward), noted,

> Every system is specifically designed to produce the results it is getting. The interconnectedness of all parts of the educational enterprise means classrooms, schools, and school districts are tied together in a web of relationships in which decisions and actions in any one part affect the other parts and the system as a whole. (p. 245)

Real change within a local educational system thus requires us to see the connections and "give attention to the interrelationships among multiple aspects of the system so that each is supportive of the others" (Cowan, 2006, p. 597).

Sashkin and Egermeier (1993) describe three traditional approaches to improvement that have shaped school reform efforts during the past half century:

- A "fix the parts" approach that focused only on strengthening key components of the education system, such as curriculum, instruction, and assessment
- A "fix the people" approach that promoted improvement only through staff training and professional development
- A "fix the school" approach that highlighted using only an organizational development perspective to improve individual schools

The authors propose that the lack of success of many educational reform efforts is attributable to exclusive emphasis on only one of these traditional approaches without the others. It is only when these three approaches are integrated and coordinated that significant and sustainable change can be expected.

SEDL'S WORKING SYSTEMICALLY: A PROCESS GROUNDED IN RESEARCH

In December 2000, the U.S. Department of Education awarded SEDL (formerly Southwest Educational Development Laboratory) a five-year contract to test a systemic approach designed to improve student achievement in reading or mathematics in low-performing districts and schools. The SEDL team drew upon more than two decades of school reform research and theory (e.g., Bossert, 1985; Hallinger & Murphy, 1986; Jenlink, Reigeluth, Carr, & Nelson, 1998; Stringfield, 1995; Teddlie & Stringfield, 1993) to identify the levels, components, and competencies of a systemic approach.

SEDL staff also investigated existing reform models that used a rational process to identify the gaps between effective and low-performing schools (Blum & Landis, 1998; Edmonds, 1979; Lezotte & Jacoby, 1992). However, it soon became apparent that many of these processes addressed only one particular gap, or problem, as it manifested itself at only one level of the system—most often at the building or classroom level. A common strategy used at that time was to find a program to fix one problem, then identify another problem and turn to another program to fix that one.

Additionally, because the underlying causes for gaps and problems were not always explored, schools typically focused on tackling the more apparent "symptoms" of their problems and failed to recognize a fundamental malfunction in the local system. As a result, the underlying problems never got "fixed" and continued to have a negative impact on schools and classrooms. This approach is like seeing water rise in a sinking boat (symptom of a problem) and merely bailing the water out (addressing the symptom) rather than trying to fix the leak (the real problem).

Testing and Refining the Working Systemically Approach

Under its contract with the U.S. Department of Education, SEDL staff worked in 23 districts and 49 schools across its five-state region—Arkansas, Louisiana, New Mexico, Oklahoma, and Texas—to test and refine the Working Systemically approach. Each of the sites in the study included the school district office and at least one school. Some of the sites were rural, some suburban, some urban. All were low performing.

In testing the Working Systemically approach, SEDL staff collected and analyzed data to design, evaluate, and refine specific steps and resources for systemic improvement (Huie, Buttram, Deviney, Murphy, & Ramos, 2004). Student achievement data were collected from partner districts and schools throughout the project. The team used a quasi-experimental design to measure student achievement gains and matched each school in the study to a composite school that represented an aggregate of similar schools in that state.

When viewed across all sites, the achievement gains were mixed, but there were encouraging results. Analyses correlating measures of systemic work and student outcomes across sites showed a statistically significant relationship between increased capacity to work systemically and student achievement in 2003 and 2004.

Results also indicated that activities related to improved alignment of curriculum, instruction, and assessment were most closely related to student achievement. Questions, therefore, began to be raised about the role of the school district in the improvement process and the need to consider the interrelated roles of individuals at multiple levels of the local system as proposed by recent studies (Murphy & Meyers, 2008; Rorrer, Skrla, & Scheurich, 2008; Thornton, Shepperson, & Canavero, 2007).

Overall, three key findings emerged from SEDL's testing of the Working Systemically approach that serve as a foundation for guiding others in the process:

- Districts and schools should stop trying to address every problem with a unique solution and focus their improvement plans on systemic strategies that are small enough to be manageable but large enough to make a difference in student achievement.

- To increase the probability of successfully improving student achievement in low-performing systems, the district needs first to concentrate its efforts on aligning curriculum, instruction, and assessment to state standards.

- Leaders at all levels of the system (including teacher leaders) need to support the selected focus for improvement so that the resources of time, personnel, and energy are targeted on that focal point.

SUMMARY

This introduction is intended as an overview of a systemic approach to district and school improvement that holds an increase in student learning as its ultimate goal. The approach is not another quick fix that addresses only a single aspect of the educational system. Rather, it provides a process for promoting a culture of continuous inquiry, networking, and collaboration, as well as structures and leadership roles that support and sustain both student and staff learning. The Working Systemically approach serves as the foundation for the systemic improvement process detailed in *Getting Serious About the System*. This guide is designed to introduce the process to teachers and other stakeholders to help them gain a basic understanding of the process and to provide an indication of what it will require on the part of district and school leaders, the entire staff, and all stakeholders to achieve this goal.

The Working Systemically Approach

Levels, Components, and Competencies

The Working Systemically approach is a multidimensional process for school improvement that focuses on key *components* of the system that need to be considered in supporting student achievement. It also identifies a core set of *competencies* that leaders in the system need to develop as they address the components. In order to ensure that the improvement is sustained over time, the approach targets multiple *levels* of the system. The goal of the Working

Figure 1 Working Systemically Dimensions

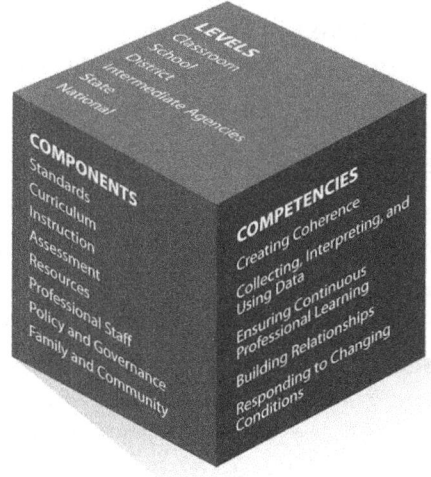

Systemically approach is to address the components and competencies at all levels, thereby resulting in systemwide improvement to increase student achievement (Cowan, Joyner, & Beckwith, 2008). These three dimensions (see Figure 1) must be considered in order to effect deep and lasting improvement.

LEVELS OF THE SYSTEM

A systems approach involves all levels of the educational enterprise (i.e., national, state, intermediate agencies, district, school, and classroom). These levels designate "the who" of the system. Improvement efforts designed to increase student achievement must be coordinated at each of these levels because each level plays a critical role in supporting and sustaining student achievement. When these levels are coordinated and working toward the same goal, they can provide a strong network of support for increased student outcomes. The six levels of the system that are integrated throughout the Working Systemically approach are described as follows:

National Level

The national level is where policy is established for federal education funding, along with guidelines for how those funds are distributed and monitored. In recent years, the national level is where dramatic steps have been taken to establish common core state standards to ensure that students across the nation are college and career ready at the end of high school. The national level also oversees large-scale data collection across the states and provides resources for dissemination of research. This level serves to focus national attention on key educational issues and ensures equal access to education.

State Level

States enact statewide educational policy; allocate funds; and prescribe mandates, guidelines, incentives, and sanctions designed to support and ensure student achievement. Some states also identify their own standards that define what students are supposed to know and be able to do at designated grade levels, as well as oversee assessments of student achievement and statewide accountability systems. Technical assistance for schools in need of improvement is also often provided through statewide efforts.

Intermediate Agency Level

Intermediate agencies (e.g., education service centers, universities) are authorized to implement initiatives assigned by the legislature or education commissioner and to assist districts and schools in operating more efficiently and effectively. Core services provided by this level of the system include training to improve instruction and program implementation, as well as special assistance to low-performing schools. Intermediate agencies also assist districts in complying with state laws and rules and with state or federal special education requirements. This level of the system provides training and assistance to teachers, administrators, members of district boards of education, and members of site-based decision-making committees.

District Level

Local policies are a vital part of improving student achievement. In addition to developing those policies, districts determine how policy is implemented and how personnel and other resources are allocated. In recent years, districts have become increasingly accountable for the learning outcomes of students in the schools within the districts. Boards of education, administrators, and district leadership teams are called upon to establish local educational priorities and help maintain the focus on improving student learning. In addition, districts create curricula aligned to common core or state standards that guide instruction and assessment at the school level.

School Level

The school level has long been the focal point for most accountability systems aimed at improving student achievement. This is the level where teachers and administrators collaborate to develop structures and processes to support teaching and learning. A primary responsibility at this level is ensuring alignment of instruction and assessment to the district curriculum. The culture established at the school level determines the extent to which structures, processes, and relationships support student and teacher growth.

Classroom Level

It is at this level where teachers create the conditions in which students can acquire the knowledge and skills prescribed by standards and curriculum documents. It is here that teachers implement instructional strategies and where students and teachers interact directly with the content. Relationships established at this level are extremely critical to the overall culture of the school and can enhance or diminish the context in which students learn.

COMPONENTS OF THE SYSTEM

The components of the Working Systemically approach represent "the what" of the system. Eight components represent the aspects of the education system on which schools, districts, and state departments of education typically focus their work. Processes that support each of the components need to be planned and coordinated with the common intention of meeting or exceeding student achievement goals.

Standards

Standards define and describe what students are expected to know and be able to do in broad terms at specific intervals of their educational experience. The present effort to establish common core state standards highlights the importance of rigorous expectations for students across the nation. Because states are increasingly aligning their assessments to these standards, an excellent starting point for beginning the improvement work is ensuring that district and school staff fully understand what students must know and be able to do to meet each standard.

Curriculum

Curriculum defines more precise district expectations of what students should know and be able to do. Ideally, the curriculum also provides a scope and sequence for learning, as well as appropriate instructional strategies and resources. A high-quality curriculum is aligned to common core or state standards and provides a road map to ensure coherence across subject areas and grade levels, making it easier for schools and teachers to organize and deliver instruction.

Instruction

Instruction is the "how" of teaching and includes the strategies used to deliver the district's curriculum. Effective teachers select evidence-based instructional strategies and ensure that their instruction addresses the needs and interests of individual students. They continually analyze the impact of their instruction on student achievement by examining student work, and they collaborate regularly to enhance their individual and collective capacity to help students achieve expected learning outcomes.

Assessment

Assessment consists of formal and informal procedures that provide teachers, schools, districts, and states a means for measuring student progress toward meeting state standards and goals set by the district and school. A viable assessment system uses multiple sources of data that measure student progress on an ongoing basis. Assessment data can also provide information about the effectiveness of specific improvement initiatives, as well as instructional strategies and resources designed to improve student performance.

Resources

Resources include financial and other assets available to a system that provide qualified and effective staff, instructional material and equipment, and facilities that support learning. Resources also include the time available for instruction, professional collaboration, and staff learning. In effective systems, decisions about resource allocation are aligned to priority district and school goals and support ongoing improvement efforts.

Professional Staff

Professional staff takes into consideration the recruitment and retention of high-quality personnel across the system. Decisions about the selection, development, and assignment of staff should reflect the needs, focus areas, and priorities of the system. As a primary resource at all levels of the system, the staff's knowledge, skill, and commitment will largely determine the successful outcome of any educational improvement initiative.

Policy and Governance

Policy and governance describe the rules and procedures—conceived at the national, state, and local levels—that are to be followed and how decisions are made to implement those rules and procedures. While policy focuses primarily on written rules and procedures, governance refers to the actions that leaders take to implement the policies and procedures. In some cases, governance is carried out by a group of individuals—the school board, for example. More frequently, it is carried out by formal and informal leaders who have responsibility for implementing policies and moving their district and schools to higher levels of performance.

Family and Community

Family and community involvement is an essential component in the educational system and can significantly contribute to the improvement work at the district, school, and classroom levels. Systems that actively seek strong family and community partnerships examine structural and psychological barriers that inhibit healthy relationships and seek multiple ways to connect to external entities to develop and reach shared goals. Positive connections among teachers, parents, schools, and the community can help identify and utilize the many available resources that schools can draw upon to support student learning.

COMPETENCIES FOR WORKING SYSTEMICALLY

School improvement approaches commonly focus on one or more of the components of the system described previously. However, without development of special competencies to work on these components, sustainable systemic improvement is not likely to occur. The Working Systemically approach focuses on building these competencies across all levels of the local system as the improvement work is conducted. Maintaining a focus on these competencies is an extremely critical aspect of building system capacity to sustain improvement over time.

Creating Coherence

Creating coherence involves taking separate parts of the system and integrating them to achieve desired outcomes (Corallo & McDonald, 2002; Newmann, Smith, Allensworth, & Bryk, 2001). Low-performing districts and schools typically respond to state and federal mandates and accountability systems in a piecemeal fashion. When a new need emerges, a new "fix" (often a new program) is found. This approach creates a fragmented system with little or no coherence among the "fixes."

With many different disconnected and incoherent reform efforts going on at once, district and school staff may work hard but become discouraged when they do not achieve desired results. Additionally, teachers and administrators often lack clarity about what the standards require students to know and be able to do. In such cases, teachers draw almost exclusively from their textbooks and personal preferences for what should be taught and assessed. Teachers are sometimes unaware of research-based instructional strategies that actively engage students in learning. Administrators may have limited knowledge of what they should be looking for in classroom visits, how professional development should be designed, and where they should allocate their limited resources.

The Working Systemically approach promotes a shared understanding of the extent to which curriculum, instruction, and assessment are aligned to standards within the local system. It involves district and school leaders actively supporting a coordinated effort and avoiding competing priorities. Through both actions and words, effective leaders continually reinforce the premise that developing successful students who can meet challenging standards is the system's top priority. Engaging stakeholders at the classroom, school, and district levels in collaborative and purposeful work to improve teaching and learning is essential for creating a coherent instructional focus.

The following questions should guide the work to build this competency in regard to alignment of curriculum, instruction, and assessment to standards—a critical aspect of a coherent system:

- Does the system have a curriculum that is aligned to state standards?
- Does the system ensure that the selection of programs and use of resources are aligned to the curriculum and student needs?
- Does the system have a curriculum scope and sequence that identifies what students should know and be able to do at each grade level?
- Does the system communicate a clear expectation that teachers use a curriculum aligned to state standards to guide their instruction?
- Does the system ensure that content expertise is available and utilized appropriately so that research-based strategies are used in the classroom?

Collecting, Interpreting, and Using Data

Collecting, interpreting, and using data is essential to making sound decisions about improving schools and districts. Identifying trends and patterns in data from multiple sources helps leaders discover underlying factors contributing to core issues and problems that need to be addressed. A deeper understanding of the nature and underlying causes of student achievement challenges in the system enables leaders to make decisions that will lead to long-term solutions.

Many districts and schools typically examine data only in the form of student test results, without exploring underlying causes of low student achievement.

As a result, they often act on hunches or beliefs that may or may not accurately represent what actually exists. This competency entails collecting data from multiple sources, arranging the data in formats that help individuals interpret them and draw conclusions, and using information from the data to take appropriate action (Bernhardt, 2004).

The Working Systemically approach calls for building the capacity of the district and school staff to collect, interpret, and use data effectively. Trends and patterns in student learning data become apparent in longitudinal arrays of data. The achievement levels of various demographic groups of students within the school and district are disaggregated to identify where strengths and weaknesses exist. Perceptual data, collected through surveys and interviews with teachers, administrators, and other stakeholders, are studied to uncover underlying attitudes and beliefs that influence action. School process data are used to determine, for example, how well district and school teams are functioning and whether professional development is affecting attitudes, beliefs, and actions. This information is crucial to effective improvement planning.

The following questions should guide the work to build this competency:

- Does the system have a process and resources for collecting and disaggregating student learning data and organizing them in understandable and useful formats?
- Does the system use multiple types of data (student achievement, demographic, perceptual, and school process) to gain a better understanding of problems and to formulate plans?
- Does the system have processes for turning data into actions that provide timely interventions for students who are not mastering the standards?

Ensuring Continuous Professional Learning

Systems that ensure continuous professional learning provide ongoing job-embedded opportunities for all staff to develop their knowledge and skills. Key elements of effective professional learning critical for sustaining improvement include

- relevance to district and school goals, needs, skill levels, and learning preferences of participants;
- a process that is long term and integrated into daily practice; and
- feedback to teachers about their progress in using the knowledge and skills learned (Mid-continent Research for Education and Learning, 2003).

Successful educational systems use multiple forms of data to identify needs of the staff for training and development. In these systems, principals participate actively in opportunities for learning and take part in planning, conducting, implementing, and evaluating professional development. Schools that understand the importance of professional learning provide adequate time for staff development and follow-up. In these schools, teachers are provided multiple opportunities for networking and receive the ongoing support and materials they need as they implement new instructional strategies.

The Working Systemically approach emphasizes professional learning that includes job-embedded opportunities for all staff to develop the knowledge and skills that are most effective for helping students achieve desired learning outcomes. The approach increases teachers' content expertise and promotes professional conversations about what to teach, how best to teach it, and how to adjust instruction to enable all students to meet the standards.

The following questions should guide the work to build this competency:

- Does the system set clear expectations for improving professional practice at all levels of the local system?
- Does the system ensure that professional learning opportunities are data driven?
- Does the system ensure that professional learning about research-based strategies is provided?
- Does the system provide adequate time for job-embedded professional learning that promotes collaboration and active participation?
- Does the system monitor the implementation and impact of new strategies and practices?

Building Relationships

Building relationships within the system does not happen serendipitously. District and school leaders must be deliberate in creating structures and processes that promote collaboration and collegiality. Ideally, teachers from different grade levels, subject areas, schools, and districts collaborate and network regularly with one another to share their knowledge, ideas, and strategies. Additionally, representatives from the school, district, families, and community work together on a common vision for improving schools.

Research demonstrates the importance of building professional relationships based on mutual respect and trust in the improvement process (Bryk & Schneider, 2002). Within a context that supports change and inquiry, individuals throughout the system create a common vision and sense of community as they undertake challenges. Professional conversations about issues related to student achievement take place in an environment in which individuals feel free to ask questions and actively listen to others, thus building strong and productive relationships in districts and schools. The fundamental purpose of such interactions is to foster a shared understanding of and commitment to improvement efforts.

Low-performing districts and schools often need structures and processes for collaboration and professional conversations. Inadequate attention to building relationships prevents district and school leaders from knowing what teachers and others need in order to implement changes in instructional practices. Additionally, teachers frequently receive mixed messages about expectations and have limited information about what is being taught or what instructional strategies are being used by other teachers in their own department or grade level.

District and school leadership teams need to provide effective structures for professional conversations and problem solving on issues central to student learning. The conversations provide insight on the needs of individuals at different levels of the system to accomplish the improvement work.

The following questions should guide the work to build this competency:

- Does the system have multiple structures and processes for individuals at different levels of the local system to have professional conversations?
- Does the system encourage positive interactions among staff members?
- Does the system encourage positive interactions among schools—both vertically and horizontally?
- Does the system encourage positive interactions between the district and the schools?
- Does the system encourage positive interactions between the district/schools and the community?

Responding to Changing Conditions

Educational systems today must adapt to myriad demographic, societal, economic, and political changes. National legislation, state accountability systems, parents, and other stakeholders exert pressure on districts and schools to change. The ability to respond effectively to changing conditions requires identifying and proactively addressing emerging or evolving issues that affect student achievement.

Typical changes that districts and schools confront include leadership transitions, resource allocation, availability of high-quality teachers, shifting demographics, state and local politics, and state and national policy. Districts and schools are better equipped to confront these and other pressures when individuals in the organization are aware of appropriate evidence-based solutions, and the organization promotes an atmosphere of continuous learning for adults as well as students.

The Working Systemically approach helps districts and schools shift from a reactive to a proactive stance and helps them make connections between changing conditions and their existing improvement efforts. Regular examination of a broad array of data helps to reveal emerging trends. This can allow staff to anticipate needed resources and explore research-based strategies to make decisions about how best to address the changing conditions.

The following questions should guide the work to build this competency:

- Does the system have processes for anticipating and recognizing changing conditions that affect multiple levels of the local system?
- Does the system promote and support innovations that help teachers and leaders respond to changing conditions?
- Does the system keep the focus on teaching and learning when conditions or circumstances change?
- Does the system seek current and relevant research and best practices to address changing conditions?

THE WORKING SYSTEMICALLY APPROACH IN ACTION

The multidimensional nature of the Working Systemically approach implies a dynamic interaction among its three aspects shown in Figure 1 on the opening page of this chapter. This book is written to provide guidance for sustainable improvement within three of the six levels of the educational system—the district, school, and classroom levels. Systemic improvement within these levels requires attention to how each of the levels affects and is affected by other levels. However, this does not mean that the national, state, and intermediate agency levels do not enter the picture. As work is being carried out at the local level, it is necessary to give attention to the national, state, and intermediate agency levels as well. For example, while the local system is often required to comply with requirements and policies at the national and state levels (e.g., national and state content and accountability standards), it can also be supported by these and other levels (e.g., intermediate agencies) through funding and access to research-based practices and technical assistance. Furthermore, intermediate agencies (e.g., education service centers, universities, social service organizations) are often called upon to provide services and technical assistance. A clear example of this interplay among the levels of the system becomes apparent in the current movement for national standards-based reform. State educational agencies and departments are increasingly called to adopt these national standards and to integrate them into their state accountability systems.

WORKING SYSTEMICALLY PHASES

This book describes, in brief, a five-phase process for implementing a systemic approach to improvement at the district, school, and classroom levels (i.e., the local system). The five phases provide a useful framework for understanding the work being done by district and school leadership teams. A more detailed description of steps in each phase, as well as specific guidance and additional

Figure 2 The Working Systemically Phases

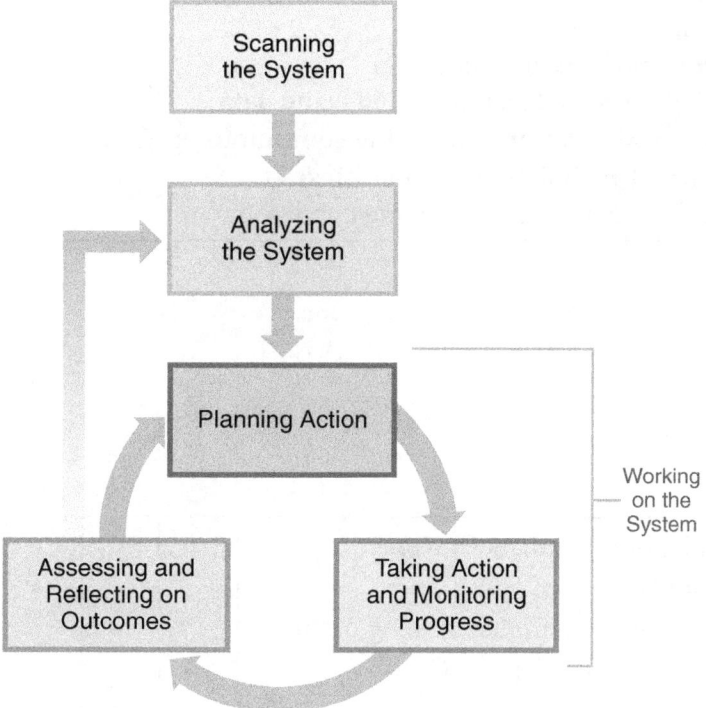

resources, may be found in *Getting Serious About the System: A Fieldbook for District and School Leaders.* These phases, and their cyclical nature, are illustrated in Figure 2.

District and school leaders develop critical competencies as they progress through each phase of the Working Systemically approach. For example, in Phase II, Analyzing the System, leaders must develop a focus for improvement (create coherence), examine data (collect, interpret, and use data), and work collaboratively with one another (build relationships).

Table 1, the Phase and Competency Correlation Matrix, provides a guide to those competencies that receive primary attention during each phase of the Working Systemically approach. However, this does not mean that only those competencies indicated are being developed during any one phase. Opportunities will emerge throughout each phase to build other competencies as well because of the multifaceted, recursive, and contextual nature of the Working Systemically approach.

Table 1   Phase and Competency Correlation Matrix

Key to competencies:

Coherence (Creating coherence)
Data (Collecting, interpreting, and using data)
Professional Learning (Ensuring continuous professional learning)
Relationships (Building relationships)
Change (Responding to changing conditions)

PHASE	Coherence	Data	Professional Learning	Relationships	Change
Phase I: Understanding Systemic Improvement Purpose: Develop an understanding of the systemic improvement process		X		X	
Phase II: Analyzing the System Purpose: Organize leadership teams that understand how the work will affect instructional practice to provide quality learning for all	X	X		X	
Phase III: Planning Action Purpose: Explore research-based strategies for providing quality learning for all and consider how actions can be incorporated into improvement plans; develop or revise improvement plan	X	X	X		X
Phase IV: Taking Action and Monitoring Implementation Purpose: Establish frameworks for meeting regularly, implementing strategies, and monitoring improvement efforts	X	X	X	X	X
Phase V: Assessing and Reflecting on Outcomes Purpose: Determine to what degree the improvement plan is being implemented and monitored; analyze actions in relation to intended outcomes	X	X		X	X

2

Phase I

Understanding Systemic Improvement

Understanding Systemic Improvement is the first of five phases described in *Getting Serious About the System*. In this phase, key leaders come to understand what systemic change is and its implications for the local district, schools, and classrooms. Leaders also review preliminary data and ensure that other key staff members at the district and school levels are committed to changes that the work may require. The phase consists of four steps:

1. Study the Approach

2. Collect and Analyze Preliminary Data

3. Present the Approach at the School Level

4. Commit to Systemic Improvement

The steps in this first phase of the work help district and school leaders embark on systemic improvement by using data to guide decision making and promoting collaborative processes. The working relationships among the district and school leaders are critical because systemic change requires a high level of collaboration, communication, and trust.

STUDY THE APPROACH

Prior to undertaking systemic improvement, key district leaders need to develop a basic understanding of what systemic improvement is, as well as the demands for effective leadership at all levels of the local system. The leaders must understand the scope of the work at the district and school levels, roles that individuals perform at these levels, and the benefits for staff and students. They consider the following expectations and commitments necessary for systemic improvement.

Stable Leadership. Systemic improvement requires a long-term commitment to educational improvement; therefore, stable leadership is vital to its success. If the superintendent or other key leaders are planning to retire or leave the district, the decision on whether or not to undertake the improvement effort should be delayed until after the transition so that the new leaders can be involved in the decision.

Authentic Involvement of Leaders. District and school leaders will need to be actively involved in the improvement process. They cannot stand on the sidelines or appoint someone else to provide leadership while they attend to routine matters. The active involvement of formal leaders, in particular, provides a powerful message about the urgency and importance of the improvement work. At the same time, formal leaders should always be attuned to ways to build leadership capacity throughout the levels of the system.

Systemwide Participation in Data Collection. Systemic improvement requires that leaders make thoughtful decisions based on multiple forms of data. Leaders must frequently engage staff members in data collection and analysis to monitor the extent to which improvement efforts are being implemented as intended, and whether these efforts are having the desired impact.

Systemwide Use of Research. Staff at all levels of the system will need to study and use current research on strategies for improvement to inform their decisions. In many cases, this will mean that long-standing practices and ways of interacting that have had little or no effect on student learning will need to be replaced with more effective ones.

Commitment to a Long-Term Improvement Effort. Implementing a complex approach that involves substantive organizational and individual change at multiple levels of a system requires a long-term commitment. During this time, district and school leaders continually develop the competencies needed to sustain improvement.

Commitment to a Systemic Approach and Goals. The improvement work requires involvement from, and a focus on, multiple levels and aspects of the system. If district and school leaders are focused on improving only a single element of the system (e.g., a single grade level, family and community involvement, or professional learning), then the improvement work ceases to be systemic in nature. In this case, another approach may be better suited to help leaders accomplish these goals.

Commitment to Supporting the Participation and Time of Teachers and Leaders. Systemic improvement requires the formation of a district leadership team to direct and monitor the improvement work. Similarly, key leaders at the school level will need to be organized and involved in implementing the improvement plan. Within the schools, teams of teachers must have time and support for collaborating on ways to improve instruction, as well as access to high-quality professional development.

Commitment to Focused, Ongoing, Job-Embedded Professional Learning for Leaders and Staff. Professional learning on the part of the adults in a system must precede increased learning on the part of students. Districts and schools characterized as learning organizations promote systemwide and school-based opportunities to integrate collaborative professional learning strategies into all their work. They also provide ongoing support and follow-up to ensure application of their learning in order to improve learning outcomes for students.

Commitment to Making the Improvement Work a Priority. The active participation and support of leaders at the district and school levels (including teacher leaders) is necessary for this effort to be effective. The fact that this work is and will continue to be a priority is a key message that needs to be communicated by leaders throughout the duration of the process.

COLLECT AND ANALYZE PRELIMINARY DATA

Leaders collect preliminary data to begin exploring the local system and to provide indicators of the potential success of the undertaking. Bernhardt's (2009) four measures of data—student learning, perceptions, demographics, and school processes—provide a useful framework for collecting and organizing data throughout the improvement process. Holcomb (2008) recommends that similar data be examined at multiple levels of the system: student performance, stakeholder perceptions, and organizational culture.

In order to be truly systemic, the improvement work should involve all schools in the district. However, because of the scope and intensity of such an approach, it is likely not feasible to implement it in more than two or three schools in the beginning. The data collected during this step will help leaders decide which schools to include in the initial work. Although student learning data are essential to make this determination, leaders should also identify initiatives already underway in the district and individual schools to decide whether the systemic approach would complement existing improvement efforts or conflict with them.

When selecting initial schools for participation, leaders consider the following factors:

Schools failing to meet national and/or state standards. This systemic improvement approach is specifically designed to improve student achievement in schools that are low performing. However, the approach can also assist schools that are already meeting or exceeding standards to work toward continuous improvement.

Schools that are linked. If district leaders select schools that are linked (e.g., represent a feeder pattern), they will be in a position to work more systemically. This allows them to address important factors—such as a K–12 scope and sequence for targeted content areas—more coherently.

Managing change. District leaders may decide to forgo selecting a school facing other significant changes (e.g., the current principal is leaving, the school will be consolidated into another school) until the situation has stabilized and any incoming leadership has an opportunity to decide whether to participate in the process.

Willing participation of school leaders. Initial resistance to major improvement work is not uncommon and may indicate a need for additional conversations before school leaders agree to participate in systemic improvement. Once the preliminary decision about the selection of schools is made, the leaders make plans to meet with principals of these recommended schools to discuss whether or not they are willing to participate.

PRESENT THE APPROACH AT THE SCHOOL LEVEL

Once the preliminary data are analyzed, the superintendent invites principals of schools under consideration to join the discussion about the systemic improvement effort. They review student achievement data and other factors that help inform the school selection process, so that principals understand why their respective schools are being considered and confirm the content areas and subgroups of students that show the greatest need for improvement as indicated by the student achievement data.

Then, in each recommended school, the principal and district leaders meet with school-level staff to inform them about the systemic improvement effort being considered by the district. Because research has shown that parent and community involvement is one of the "essential supports" necessary for school reform (Bryk, Sebring, Allensworth, Luppescu, & Easton, 2010), this meeting should also include parent and community leaders. The meeting provides an opportunity to explain why the school has been selected for the initial improvement work. It also allows participants to ask questions and express any concerns over the proposed work.

COMMIT TO
SYSTEMIC IMPROVEMENT

After the school meetings, the superintendent and other district leaders meet with the principals again and decide whether or not to implement the systemic improvement process. In making their decision, leaders consider the questions and concerns expressed at the school meetings in addition to the data they have collected to date. This information and feedback from the staff helps them to know whether the schools initially selected for the improvement work are ready and willing to begin.

The superintendent ensures that everyone involved has a clear understanding of the nature of the work and specific commitments involved in implementing the improvement effort. To build support and commitment throughout the local system, additional district leaders, principals, school board members, parents, and community members may be involved in this decision.

3

Phase II

Analyzing the System

Analyzing the System is the second of five phases in the systemic improvement process. The purpose of Phase II is to establish membership of district and school leadership teams and identify systemic issues—through a comprehensive needs assessment—that are hindering student achievement. In this phase, the district and school leaders increase their understanding of how the work will directly affect the system as a whole, including instructional practice in the classroom. Analyzing the System consists of eight steps:

1. Form the District and School Leadership Teams

2. Begin the Comprehensive Needs Assessment

3. Conduct a Gap Analysis

4. Begin the Process at the School Level

5. Formulate Problem Statements

6. Describe the Ideal State

7. Review District Initiatives

8. Continue the Process at the School Level

Analyzing the System helps district and school leaders begin to take focused, deliberate steps toward understanding their local system as it currently exists. This phase introduces processes for organizing the leadership team, investigating research-based practices, and using data to make decisions.

FORM THE DISTRICT AND SCHOOL LEADERSHIP TEAMS

Having committed to systemic improvement, the superintendent and key leaders select members of the district leadership team. Key professional staff may need to be added to the initial group of leaders to ensure essential levels, roles, and perspectives in the system are represented. Key functions of the district team include the following:

- Establishing and maintaining the focus for the improvement effort
- Creating and regularly updating the district improvement plan
- Monitoring implementation of the district improvement plan throughout the school year
- Ensuring that necessary support and resources are provided so that staff members can implement the plan effectively
- Ensuring that the improvement effort is—and remains—a system priority
- Assessing outcomes of the work and adjusting plans accordingly

This team will coordinate and support the improvement effort at the district level as the work evolves. The district leaders select members based on the local context and the analysis of preliminary data from Phase I. In addition, those making the selection of district team members consider the following roles:

- **Informal leaders.** District leaders need to look beyond formal positions or titles and consider individuals who are informal leaders and whose input and support would be an asset to the team. Often these individuals bring viewpoints to the planning process that help tailor a plan for a particular system. Additionally, informal leaders to whom district- and school-level staff turn for information and guidance can help emphasize the importance of the improvement effort, communicate district team deliberations, and build support among staff members throughout the system.

- **Leaders from schools in the same feeder pattern.** The district improvement plan places a priority on aligning the curriculum, instruction, and assessment to common core or state standards. This often means creating or revising the district curriculum and including an instructional scope and sequence for each grade level in the target schools. The results may have substantial implications for instructional planning at those schools. Principals in the feeder pattern should be involved in shaping the district plan to ensure that student progress from one grade level to the next is as smooth and efficient as possible.

- **Representatives from other schools.** It is recommended that principals and leaders from schools other than those directly targeted for the initial work also serve on the district leadership team.

Their involvement helps prepare them for active participation in the improvement process in the future.

- **Individuals with specialized knowledge or experience.** The district leaders identify individuals in the system who have expertise in content areas or experience with special populations of students. They should also consider individuals who are familiar with existing initiatives in the district. These members would help ensure that the district improvement plan does not overlook any student populations and takes into consideration existing improvement efforts. The addition of a person who has skills in data collection and analysis could assist with formatting data to help the whole team make informed decisions.

- **Other stakeholders, such as parents, community members, and board members.** These individuals can often provide important perspectives existing outside the system. Effective family and community engagement is an important aspect of systemic improvement and can result in improved student achievement, as well as greater communitywide support for districts and schools. In addition to their official capacity as policymakers, school board members are often in a position to communicate to the community at large and build public support for major improvement initiatives. Involving representation from these constituencies helps promote shared responsibility for student learning.

Once the leadership team members have been identified and their participation confirmed, they meet to discuss what it means to work systemically. They also establish the purpose of the team and how it will function. The team then formulates guidelines for how the team will work together through the following activities:

- Identifying norms for working together. Norms provide guidelines for how the team members will interact, make decisions, and conduct business. They are an important aspect in establishing a culture of collaboration and continuous professional learning, as well as ensuring that meetings are productive and emotionally safe.
- Establishing the purpose and organization of the team. The members of the leadership team serve as liaisons to different groups within the system. Therefore, it is important that they can articulate the purpose of the team and how it will affect the district (or school). Team members should also clarify members' roles and agree on procedures for team meetings, including how often they will meet and their schedule of meetings for the remainder of the school year. They should also determine how long they are expected to serve on the team and how they will make decisions. Establishing a clear understanding of these issues will help orient members to their individual and collective roles and prepare them to work together as a team.

A recurring function of the district leadership team will be to examine periodically the composition of the team in relation to the specific focus of the

Figure 3 The Systemic Planning Process

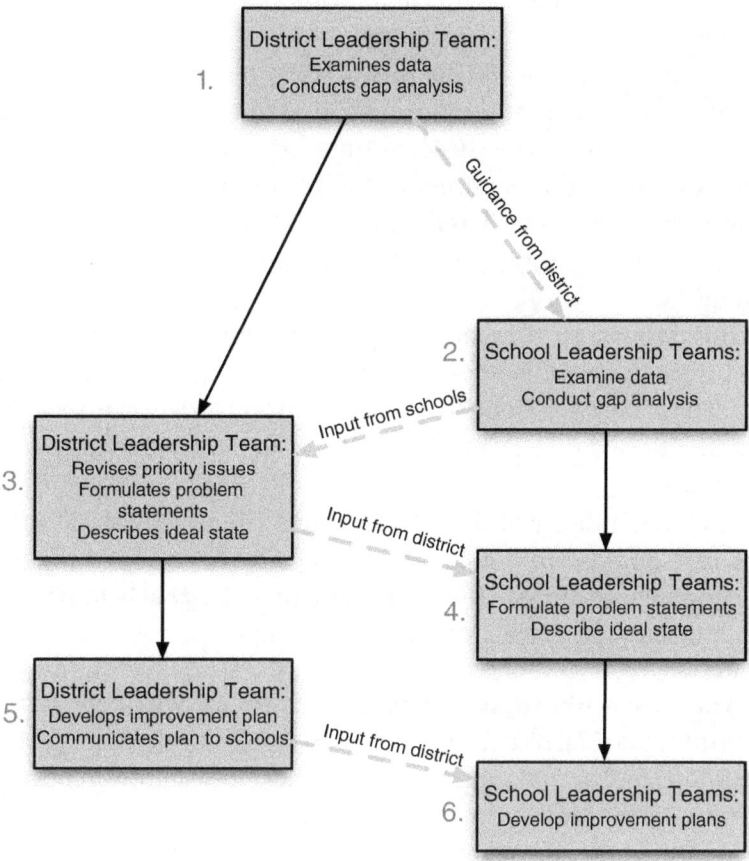

improvement work and adjust it accordingly. Each participating school repeats the process of forming a leadership team and establishing the team's purpose and guidelines for their meetings. In addition to the principal, membership roles that should be considered for the school teams include informal leaders, individuals with specialized knowledge or experience, and family and community representatives. Figure 3, Systemic Planning Process, illustrates how the work proceeds from the district team to the school teams, with input to and from each other.

BEGIN THE COMPREHENSIVE NEEDS ASSESSMENT

A critical step in systemic improvement is conducting a comprehensive needs assessment (CNA). The CNA reveals both strengths and challenges in various areas of the district or school. It is a process that should be repeated at least annually to determine where progress is being made and to highlight areas that still need to be addressed. The leadership team begins the CNA process by examining resources that explain the importance of collecting and analyzing multiple types of data. As mentioned earlier, Holcomb's (2008) data categories and Bernhardt's (2009) multiple measures of data can be used as possible resources for learning.

It is recommended that the team initially collect three years of student achievement data and information from the System Alignment Survey, interviews, and focus groups. The System Alignment Survey is designed to elicit perceptual data about the alignment of curriculum, instruction, and assessment to state standards, as well as the availability of resources and professional development to support improvement. This information will be used later in the gap analysis.

The primary purpose of the interviews and focus groups is to hear perceptions about initiatives, professional development, alignment, and other areas relevant to school improvement. The leadership team identifies a sample of professional staff who would be most appropriate to participate in the interviews and focus groups.

Because confidentiality and trust are issues when individuals are asked to share their perceptions, an outside facilitator may be engaged to conduct the interviews and focus groups. The facilitator's primary role is to stimulate honest and open discussion in relation to the following:

- **Perceptions about the students.** Participants often share existing attitudes and beliefs about students in the district/school that influence decisions and actions and determine expectations for achievement outcomes. These perceptions also provide insight into the organizational and individual efficacy existing in the system to address challenging learning needs of students.

- **Current improvement programs, initiatives, or interventions.** Information and opinions about existing school improvement initiatives can help leaders determine whether any new initiative will complement those programs or compete for district resources. Existing content-area programs and initiatives may require district and school staff to spread themselves too thinly to implement the systemic work effectively. This information is important because, later in this phase, district leaders will select a focus for their improvement work.

- **Alignment of curriculum, instruction, and assessment to common core or state standards.** Descriptions of current and past efforts to align local curriculum, instruction, and assessment to standards can provide information about factors in the system that promote success and present challenges. Of particular interest are ongoing processes for supporting teachers, as well as steps taken to monitor the implementation and impact of alignment. The degree to which steps have been taken to ensure this critical alignment will be a major factor in determining initial improvement efforts.

- **Nature of professional learning.** It is useful for the leadership team to understand school leaders' awareness about the characteristics of effective professional learning and the extent to which data are used to determine professional learning needs. Participant responses will also provide information about when professional learning opportunities are available throughout the school year and the school day and reveal how well the district is guiding and supporting the implementation of new instructional strategies.

- **Opportunities for interaction and collaboration.** The team needs to know the extent to which district and school staff interact productively—both individually and organizationally—to increase student achievement. Systemic improvement requires regular and frequent collaboration among and between formal leaders and instructional staff across and within grade levels and content areas. Questions in this area are likely to reveal expectations for collaboration, how collaboration is supported and monitored, and successes and challenges in this area.

- **Communication strategies.** The manner and effectiveness in which information and priorities are communicated are important factors in shaping district and school culture. Understanding the nature of existing communication will help the leadership team maintain strategies that function well or adopt more effective ones.

- **Current structures for planning and implementing the improvement work.** Information about formal and informal structures for promoting shared decision making, identifying school priorities, using data, planning action, and monitoring implementation and impact is critical to understanding a school's context. The team needs to know whether existing structures, such as school-level improvement teams, are operating effectively and focused consistently on teaching and learning. Participant responses will reveal whether existing structures, such as district- and school-level leadership teams, are operating effectively and focused consistently on teaching and learning. The degree to which the local system is organized to increase student achievement will influence the team's choice of how to begin the improvement work.

Organizing data from the CNA into understandable formats is an important aspect of the work at this point because it enables team members to interpret their data during the gap analysis process. Creating charts, graphs, and tables can help the staff see trends and patterns in their data and allows them to draw informed conclusions about conditions in the district and school.

CONDUCT A GAP ANALYSIS

The gap analysis is a process that helps leadership teams compare conditions and practices in their district and schools to those in high-performing districts and schools. The process requires someone to act as facilitator who will gather necessary data and other materials, create data sets for team members, and guide the team through the process.

In the first step of the process, before they examine their data, members of the leadership team make predictions about what the data will reveal and explore possible assumptions that underlie those predictions. They then review state and federal requirements for proficiency under the current accountability systems. Team members next review collected data (organized into charts, graphs, and tables) and look for patterns and trends within subgroups of students, content areas in greatest need of improvement, and consistencies and inconsistencies across the different data sources. They make note of important findings that "pop out" of the data. The team then conducts a gap analysis that helps compare conditions and practices in the local system to those in high-performing systems using the System Examination Tool (Appendix I), which is organized around the eight systemic components (curriculum, instruction, assessment, standards, resources, professional staff, policy and governance, and family and community). The gap analysis process helps the team identify the most important elements in the local system that need to be strengthened during the initial improvement work.

BEGIN THE PROCESS AT THE SCHOOL LEVEL

The leadership team at each of the participating schools duplicates the activities completed by the district team in beginning the CNA and conducting the gap analysis. After the school teams make predictions about what their data will show and review their data, they use the System Examination Tool to complete the gap analysis, using conditions at their school as their primary reference point. They then summarize the challenges they identified and submit them to the district team to consider in the formulation of district problem statements.

FORMULATE PROBLEM STATEMENTS

Before formulating a problem statement, the district leadership team engages in a discussion about the major issues that emerged from the gap analysis at both the district and school levels. The focus of the discussion is on what those issues indicate in terms of a problem that exists in the system and how these problems affect student achievement. District leaders consider the summaries of challenges submitted by the schools and determine whether any of those issues should be addressed by the district leadership team rather than only at the school level. The team consolidates the highest priority systemic issues identified in the gap analysis into one to three problem statements that will focus the initial work in the improvement effort.

The leadership team then examines research and best practices relevant to the identified problems. This process will help the team articulate how they envision the system functioning once the problems have been addressed.

DESCRIBE THE IDEAL STATE

Describing the ideal state involves a series of actions designed to help the district leadership team refine and narrow the scope of the improvement work to make it more specific and manageable. The team reviews the problem statements and begins transforming them into the ideal state, which will focus on critical issues. A key question guiding the discussion at this point is, "Since the problem statements highlight the issues we want to address, how would we describe this system if the problems were completely solved?"

REVIEW SYSTEM INITIATIVES

The leadership team reviews and maps out current initiatives already existing within the system. They reflect on whether the current initiatives are designed to help achieve the ideal state just described. They then determine which initiatives need to be kept or redesigned, and which can be eliminated.

After reviewing existing initiatives, the leadership team refocuses on the systemic approach to improvement work. The team reflects on the interrelationships they have discovered among the problems they identified and their current improvement initiatives, as well as the district and school status on the components and competencies of the approach revealed by the gap analysis.

Throughout this process, it is important to establish strategies for maintaining regular and effective communication between the district and school levels. Therefore, the district leadership team develops a plan for communicating throughout the system the progress the team has made, as well as their problem statements and description of the ideal state. This communication should include a brief description of important findings and decisions and how they relate to specific components and competencies of the systemic improvement approach.

CONTINUE THE PROCESS
AT THE SCHOOL LEVEL

The leadership team at each participating school duplicates the processes used by the district team in formulating their own problem statements and describing the ideal state. The teams also examine existing initiatives that have been adopted in their respective schools and determine which ones are likely to aid in achieving the ideal state and which may hinder the process. Team members then refocus on the systemic process and reflect on the competencies they have been developing to help sustain school improvements once they have been implemented.

4

Phase III

Planning Action

Planning Action is the third of five phases in systemic improvement. In Phase III, leaders reflect on what research shows to be effective practices for increasing student achievement and consider how those practices can be incorporated into the improvement effort. Leadership teams gain more insight into the status of their existing district or school improvement plan and the process used to develop it. Each team revises or develops a detailed plan that lays out the goals, objectives, strategies, and action steps, as well as the necessary monitoring and support. Planning Action consists of six steps:

1. Investigate Research-Based Practices
2. Explore the Professional Teaching and Learning Cycle (PTLC)
3. Review Progress Made to Date and Existing Plan
4. Develop a District Improvement Plan
5. Formalize and Communicate the District Improvement Plan
6. Develop School Improvement Plans

Once the Planning Action phase of the work is completed, leaders and staff members at all levels have detailed plans that map out the work ahead and the tools necessary for implementing and monitoring the work in the next phase.

INVESTIGATE RESEARCH-BASED PRACTICES

In this process, leadership teams become aware of research-based and promising practices to ensure that well-developed improvement plans are implemented and that the plans have a positive impact on student achievement. It is important for a team to look carefully at research and best practices before developing an improvement plan. Team members need to know what practices have been shown by research to improve student performance and to incorporate into their plan those practices that may help in solving the problems they have identified.

Pertinent areas of research may include the following:

- Alignment of curriculum, instruction, and assessment to standards. Because alignment is a school-level factor highly associated with increased student achievement, it should be an initial consideration for school improvement.
- Ongoing, job-embedded professional learning. Professional learning should not be a one-time event that occurs isolated from any ongoing effort; it is an integral and essential aspect of systemic change. It must be ongoing, standards based, and results driven.
- Leadership roles to support implementation. Leadership at all levels of the system must support implementation of new practices. Effective leaders assume responsibility for communicating clear expectations, building capacity, and monitoring and reviewing.

The leadership team may also examine characteristics of low-performing districts/schools identified by researchers (Chenowith, 2007; Cohen & Ginsburg, 2001; Corallo & McDonald, 2002) and then discuss the extent to which they are apparent in the local system:

- Extremely low standards and expectations for students
- Very little use of data to identify and solve specific problems
- Limited capacity for implementing improvement efforts
- Inadequate knowledge of quality instruction
- Less experienced and less qualified teachers and other instructional staff
- High staff absenteeism and turnover rates
- Inadequate leadership for substantive change
- Atmosphere of distrust, disrespect, and barely controlled chaos
- Low morale

EXPLORE THE PROFESSIONAL TEACHING AND LEARNING CYCLE (PTLC)

The PTLC is an ongoing, job-embedded process for professional learning focused on alignment of curriculum, instruction, and assessment to standards.

Figure 4 The PTLC Steps, Leadership Roles, and Culture

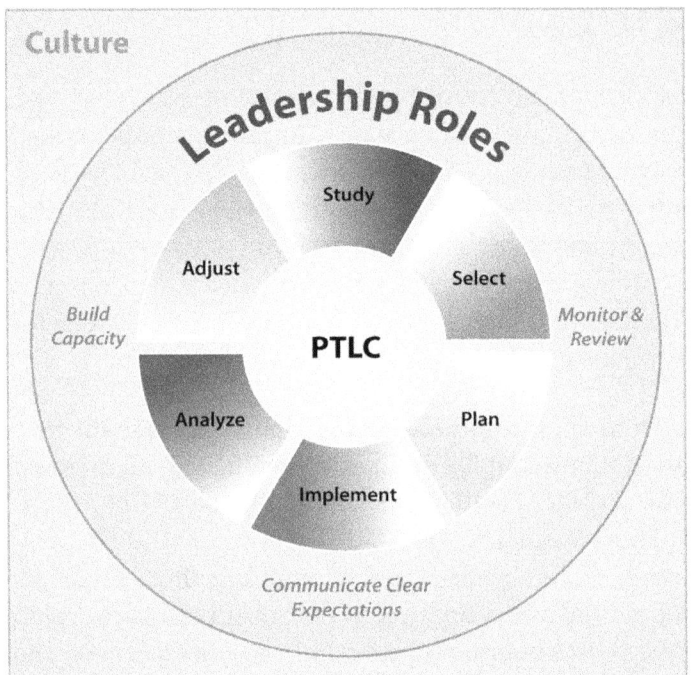

It uses a lesson-study process and is specifically designed to promote alignment and collaboration through the examination of research-based instructional practices and student work. The PTLC is a valuable strategy for improving a system's capacity to increase student achievement and extending the systemic work to the classroom level.

The PTLC process begins with an examination of data to identify a specific content-area focus. An item analysis of student achievement results in that content area provides information about which of the specific learning expectations from the common core or state standards should be addressed first. The following provides a brief description of the six steps of PTLC.

Step 1. Study

Teachers work in collaborative planning teams (grade level, vertical, or departmental) to examine the learning expectations from the selected state standards; they also review how those expectations are assessed on the state assessment.

Step 2. Select

Collaborative planning teams research and select instructional strategies and resources for enhancing learning as described in the standards.

Step 3. Plan

Planning teams, working together, develop a common lesson incorporating the selected strategies, and they agree on the type of student work teachers will use as evidence of student learning in Step 5 (Analyze).

Step 4. Implement

Teachers teach the planned lesson, making note of implementation successes and challenges, and gather the agreed-upon evidence of student learning.

Step 5. Analyze

Teachers meet again in collaborative teams to examine student work and reflect on student performance as an indicator of instructional effectiveness.

Step 6. Adjust

Collaborative teams reflect on the implications of the analysis of student work. Teachers discuss alternative instructional strategies or modifications to the original instructional strategy that would enhance student learning.

The PTLC requires three leadership roles to support implementation: communicating clear expectations, building capacity, and monitoring and reviewing. The following is a brief synopsis of the leadership roles.

Communicating Clear Expectations

In communicating clear expectations, leaders at all levels of the local system do the following:

- Regularly communicate expectations in both actions and words
- Frequently discuss priorities related to student achievement to a wide audience
- Actively participate in meetings and professional learning sessions to communicate their importance and value

Building Capacity

To build capacity, leaders at all levels of the local system do the following:

- Support collaborative learning at all levels of the system
- Provide for time, space, and resources needed for staff to learn how to increase student learning
- Regularly engage in personal professional learning for effective teaching and learning

Monitoring and Reviewing

In monitoring and reviewing, leaders at all levels of the local system do the following:

- Regularly and frequently monitor implementation and impact of initiatives
- Engage others in collecting and analyzing data to assess implementation and impact of improvement initiatives
- Regularly and frequently use different forms of data to make decisions

A collaborative culture at all levels of the system is vital to the implementation of the PTLC. The process requires teachers to engage in frequent meetings with grade-level or content-area colleagues in which they critically examine their instructional practices and explore more effective teaching strategies. The PTLC also requires a strong commitment to the process on the part of leaders.

As the team members develop their improvement plan, they incorporate action steps to implement the PTLC. Leadership actions for supporting and monitoring implementation of each step of the PTLC are also included in the plan.

REVIEW PROGRESS MADE TO DATE AND EXISTING PLAN

The district leadership team reviews the accomplishments and decisions made in the first two phases. This information will guide development of the improvement plan.

The review includes the following points:

- A summary of the collected data
- The outcomes of the gap analysis
- The team's problem statements
- The ideal state

The leadership team examines the current plan in light of their study of research and best practices and discusses the extent to which it is designed to solve the identified problems. The review also reveals the district's/school's past success in implementing and monitoring its plans.

The team discusses several questions when reviewing the plan:

- **How was the plan developed?** This information will reveal the extent to which the district and school improvement plans were collaboratively developed. It also brings out information about how data were used to identify district and school needs and whether the planning was a deliberate process, or was done only to satisfy state or federal requirements.

- **Does the plan map out a clear course of action centered on using research-based practices?** The team examines the extent to which the plan reflects research-based strategies and provides clear direction about who will take which actions and by when.

- **Does the plan identify professional learning required for implementation?** The team discusses whether the district and schools developed a process for identifying the skills and knowledge that staff members need in order to implement actions in the improvement plan. The team also determines to what degree the district and schools have followed through and provided for those needs.

- **Does the plan allocate sufficient resources for priorities and initiatives?** The team determines whether the district and schools have provided adequate resources (e.g., time, money, and staff) to address identified needs and implement multiple priorities and initiatives effectively.

- **Is there a process for monitoring the implementation and impact of strategies?** The team reflects on the district's and schools' history of implementing improvement plans and determines whether the current plan includes a clear process for regularly checking on progress in carrying out the actions in the plan. This process should include a specific timeline for monitoring both implementation and impact of individual strategies. The team identifies the data sources used to measure whether the strategies were implemented and whether they achieved desired outcomes.

The leadership team also analyzes how the plan addresses issues related to the problem statements and ideal state. Parts of the existing plan that are relevant to the identified problems might be modified or strengthened during the development of the new improvement plan.

DEVELOP A DISTRICT IMPROVEMENT PLAN

To begin the process of developing (or revising) an improvement plan, the team members review their problem statements and confirm the ideal state they have described. These are then used to identify the goals and objectives that will serve as the framework for the plan. The leadership team should establish one to two goals that address the most important issues that surfaced during the gap analysis. For each goal, the team creates one to three objectives that will lead to attaining that goal.

The team next identifies strategies and action steps to complete the improvement plan. It takes another important, but often overlooked, step in determining for each strategy

- evidence that will demonstrate that the strategy was completed (evidence of implementation) and
- evidence that will demonstrate that the strategy had any effect on moving toward the ideal state (evidence of impact).

In addition, for each action step, the team determines

- the person(s) ultimately responsible for carrying out each action step,
- resources needed to implement the action step,
- the date by which the step should be completed, and
- a timeline that specifies when the action step will be reviewed.

The team members study the descriptions of the leadership roles and use the Leadership Self-Assessment tool (Appendix II) that guides them in determining specific leadership action steps for the improvement plan. The tool also helps them identify where leadership capacity must be built to carry out the plan. The team members examine their own strengths and weaknesses in the leadership roles and reflect on them at intervals throughout the year to monitor their growth in the three roles.

The team identifies specific dates for reviewing the improvement plan, particularly the evidence of implementation and impact. It is recommended that the team review the plan at least quarterly. As the plan is being implemented and monitored, the leadership team may see the need for adjustments to the plan. In some cases, action steps in the original plan will need to be revised; in other cases, steps may need to be deleted, added, or extended in time. These changes will be noted in the plan during the reviews and communicated throughout the system. The team will track changes to the plan and ensure that the improvement plan remains a living document that actively guides the work.

A key step in planning the improvement work is to place important items from the plan on the district and school calendar for the year ahead. Team members schedule

- monthly meetings of the leadership team,
- regular reviews of the improvement plan,
- progress updates to schools, and
- professional development sessions.

FORMALIZE AND COMMUNICATE THE DISTRICT IMPROVEMENT PLAN

The school board, as the governing body of the school district, needs to understand the nature and extent of the work to be undertaken in the implementation of the district improvement plan. The school board can be instrumental in setting policies, ensuring that needed resources are available, and communicating the district focus to the larger community. The district team prepares and presents the finalized plan to the school board. A summary of the district team's comprehensive needs assessment, the problem statements, and the ideal state should be included in this presentation, as well as a brief explanation of the following key points:

- How the plan was developed with input from staff members at all levels
- How the district plan will be implemented
- How the district will keep the improvement effort a long-term priority
- How school improvement plans will be developed
- How district and school plans will be mutually supportive

Although a school leadership team will guide the improvement efforts at the school level, all staff need to be aware of the district plan. District-team representatives from each of the participating schools determine how to communicate the district improvement plan to their respective school staff. In addition to the key points provided to the school board, the following information is communicated in this meeting:

- Explanation of how needs/challenges identified by the participating schools were taken into consideration in developing the district plan
- Emphasis that implementation of the district and school plans will be a priority at the district level, demonstrating that the system is taking proactive steps to improve student achievement and serve all the students in the district
- Summary of the next steps that will occur, primarily the development of the school improvement plan
- Recognition of school representatives on the district leadership team, reinforcing that representation from all levels of the local system was instrumental in the plan development

DEVELOP SCHOOL IMPROVEMENT PLANS

A key aspect of creating coherence in a system is ensuring that improvement plans at the district and school levels are mutually supportive. Each school leadership team reviews its ideal state and determines whether revisions are needed so that the school's improvement work supports the district's priorities. The school team then develops its own improvement plan—following the same procedure used by the district team. During the development of the school plan, the team consults the district plan to ensure alignment of the two plans.

Of critical importance is the understanding that meaningful change in student performance will not occur until the improvement work reaches the classroom level. Also, as in the district plan, monitoring implementation and impact of strategies is crucial and must not be omitted from the plan.

Once the school improvement plan has been completed, the leadership team submits the plan to the district leadership team for review. If no revisions are suggested, the school team continues with the next step, presenting the plan to the school staff.

The leadership team next decides how to communicate the details of the school improvement plan to teachers and other staff members at the school and classroom levels. It is important for all staff to recognize that the school plan and the district plan are mutually supportive. Another key point should be the collaborative nature of the plan development, with input provided from school-level staff in the development of the district's improvement plan as well as their own.

Leaders emphasize that implementation of both the district and school plans will be given high priority at appropriate levels of the system and also that active participation by all staff will be expected and encouraged. Finally, the team explains what the next steps will be in implementing the plan.

5

Phase IV

Taking Action and Monitoring Progress

Taking Action and Monitoring Progress is the fourth of five phases in the systemic improvement approach. In Phase IV, staff members carry out the planned actions at the district, school, and classroom levels. Individuals at each level have responsibilities for implementing the improvement plan.

District and school leaders monitor—both formally and informally—strategies implemented, evaluate the impact of those strategies, and review the next steps to determine whether modifications need to be made to the improvement plan. Leaders communicate any changes to the plan throughout the system, ensure that necessary resources will be available, and build capacity to carry out the work. Staff members take action and the improvement work continues.

It should be noted that the three steps of Phase IV are not linear in nature. The first step establishes the structure that will guide the implementation process; the second and third ones recur throughout the improvement work wherever necessary:

1. Implement and Monitor the Improvement Plans

2. Provide Continuing Leadership for the Improvement Work

3. Address Unique Challenges as They Arise

IMPLEMENT AND MONITOR THE IMPROVEMENT PLANS

In this step, the district and school leadership teams begin implementing their respective improvement plans. These plans map out who will carry out what actions and by when. Members of the district and school leadership teams provide encouragement, guidance, and support to those responsible for implementation throughout the improvement process.

As implementation begins, challenges and frustrations are likely to occur, especially when individuals and groups are asked to change long-established behaviors and practices. Staff members often experience confusion and anxiety, and the strong professional relationships that are being forged will help alleviate such feelings. Leaders may face a challenge in maintaining focus and momentum throughout the course of the improvement process. Leadership teams play a critical role in keeping commitment to improvement in the spotlight.

Sustaining the improvement work over time requires leaders to maintain frequent contact with the staff members carrying out the action steps. Regular meetings with those staff members are essential not only for guiding the work and gaining information about needs, but also for providing opportunities to acknowledge progress and offer encouragement and support. Planning and actively participating in leadership team meetings and professional development communicates leaders' commitment to improvement efforts.

Leadership teams play a critical role in maintaining the focus and commitment on the established plan in face of these distractions. The regular team meetings provide the structure and process needed to guide implementation of the improvement plan. Thoughtful and intentional planning of these meetings significantly affects the success of the effort. Scheduling meetings on at least a monthly basis helps ensure that the improvement work remains a priority throughout the system. Regular meetings also provide opportunities to monitor the work closely and respond to changing conditions.

As emphasized earlier, it is important for leadership teams to establish and abide by a set of norms and guidelines for meetings, and leadership teams integrate them into the meeting process. It is possible that norms and guidelines established earlier may require adjustments to accommodate the focus of more current meetings.

As the team begins to implement the improvement plan, members review recently completed actions and discuss how they were implemented and what happened as a result. They discuss the challenges and successes that they experienced or observed and also reflect on circumstances and factors that led to those challenges or successes.

Members also report on current actions and recognize milestones reached. They review any new data and discuss current challenges they are encountering, as well as ideas for overcoming these challenges. Leaders should consider how to provide support for the work, including providing professional learning, allocating necessary resources, and addressing challenges as they arise. Regularly reviewing data in these areas is an effective strategy for identifying critical needs.

Building in reflection time at the end of meetings helps team members process new insights and explore how to improve meetings. This time also provides an opportunity to reinforce the primary goal of improving student achievement.

PROVIDE CONTINUING LEADERSHIP FOR THE IMPROVEMENT WORK

During Phase IV, as implementation of the plan begins, it is crucial for leaders at every level of the local system to assume responsibility for all aspects of the improvement work. Leaders build their capacity to plan, implement, and support strategies and processes necessary to carry out the work in schools, particularly at the classroom level.

Part of the capacity building may include developing the knowledge and skills needed to monitor the improvement work. For example, administrators need to monitor the implementation of research-based instructional strategies. This requires regular visits to classrooms, with a defined focus for the visits. Because monitoring is crucial for successful implementation of any new initiative, leaders must perform this function.

Leaders also consider how to provide support for the work, including providing for the professional learning needs of staff, allocating necessary resources, and addressing challenges as they arise. By regularly reviewing data in these areas, they are able to identify critical needs in a timely way. As the district and school staff begin to implement their improvement plans, they consider key questions such as these:

- What questions do staff have about aspects of the plan and what clarifications are needed?
- What issues do leaders need to address in order to sustain progress and momentum? How should they address these issues?
- What professional learning or resource needs do staff members have? How should leaders provide for these needs?
- Are there areas in which additional support is needed? How should leaders provide this support?

Keeping a long-term effort a priority for its duration can be extraordinarily difficult, especially in an environment with many competing, and sometimes conflicting, demands. The district and school leadership teams play crucial roles in keeping the goals a priority at all levels of the system. Leadership teams detail their communication strategies and incorporate them into district and school improvement plans. Among actions that leaders take to communicate clear expectations are the following:

- **Stating explicitly that this work is—and will remain—a priority.** Effective leaders build this message into their communication throughout the school year—in speech, in writing, and in action. Delivering this message clearly and frequently is a powerful way leaders increase commitment of staff members and obtain results.

- **Reiterating the long-term nature of the work.** An inconsistent approach sends conflicting messages about whether or not the work is indeed a priority. Without this constant reminder, staff members may feel that they are not really responsible for implementing the improvement plan or that the work will no longer be a priority the following year.

- **Maintaining open communication with all stakeholders.** In order for the improvement work to remain systemic, individuals at all levels must be informed of key decisions made and accomplishments achieved. They should also have multiple opportunities to provide input into decisions and to understand how these decisions will affect their work. Communicating with other important stakeholders, such as families and community groups, adds valuable perspectives and helps broaden understanding and commitment to the improvement work.

District and school leaders ensure that staff members develop the knowledge and skills required to implement the improvement plan. Particularly important is the ability to use data to inform decisions. The leaders regularly review implementation and impact evidence from the improvement plans and collect additional data when needed. This review process, at both the district and school levels, frequently reveals the need for resources or professional learning among the instructional staff or the leaders themselves.

From time to time, leaders must make adjustments to the improvement plan(s) based on an understanding of evolving staff needs. For example, working collaboratively on the common core or state standards or district curriculum may require new knowledge and skills in instructional or assessment strategies. Building the capacity of staff to do the improvement work is a fundamental part of providing leadership and, ultimately, increasing student achievement.

An additional consideration for building capacity is the allocation of needed resources to implement the improvement plan. These resources include the personnel to complete planned actions (e.g., content specialists), staff time (e.g., for collaboration in the PTLC), and funds needed to support the work (e.g., purchase of instructional materials). Although these elements may be specified in the improvement plan, leaders remain flexible in resource allocation as they respond to changing conditions. Consistently providing appropriate resources as the work evolves helps maintain momentum and communicates to staff members that their efforts are supported and valued and that this work remains a top priority.

Monitoring implementation and impact of the strategies in the improvement plan is a critical part of systemic improvement. Information gained from regular and frequent reviews of the plan helps guide decisions about how best to direct the work and support the individuals responsible for implementation.

Because monitoring occurs both formally and informally, leaders must be familiar with both approaches for collecting data. Informal monitoring may occur in day-to-day conversations with the individuals carrying out the plan. This proactive approach communicates that the work is a priority and provides immediate information about challenges and issues.

Formal monitoring is more structured in nature and sometimes requires data collection tools or protocols. Leaders at the district and school levels should schedule formal reviews of the progress made to date by those individuals charged with carrying out aspects of the improvement plan. These reviews, which should occur at least quarterly, provide valuable information for decisions about adjustments to the improvement plans and timelines. In each formal review session, participants

- review the planned actions that were scheduled to be completed by the established dates and determine whether they were accomplished,
- identify what supported the successfully completed actions and what will help sustain the momentum, and
- identify challenges and issues that prevented successful completion of strategies and determine steps needed to accomplish these tasks.

The leadership team clarifies how to address emerging issues. Monitoring implementation requires leaders to track progress so they can adjust the planned actions and accomplish goals more effectively. However, they also recognize that the term "monitoring" may carry negative connotations. Staff may perceive monitoring with concern, for example, if they believe that leaders are actually evaluating their individual performances, checking whether or not they are doing their jobs, or investigating their abilities. Without actions to convince them otherwise, these misconceptions may contribute to a culture of distrust and ultimately reduce the overall effectiveness of the improvement effort. Helping staff members view monitoring in a positive sense, especially early in the work, may be done by

- clarifying that monitoring of the plan is a means of checking progress, not evaluating individuals;
- explaining how and why monitoring plays a critical role in implementing an improvement plan;
- emphasizing how monitoring implementation of the plan is different from evaluating the performance of individuals; and
- detailing why and how monitoring will occur, particularly at the classroom level.

ADDRESS UNIQUE
CHALLENGES AS THEY ARISE

Every school system is unique, and a distinctive combination of factors influences how educational stakeholders perceive, describe, and implement an improvement effort. Challenges and needs that are specific to a particular system emerge as the work unfolds. For a process of this magnitude to be effective, leaders must provide ongoing support that is tailored to the unique culture, capacity, and needs of the system. Anticipating challenges before they arise and addressing emergent issues in a timely manner helps ensure that the work continues to move forward and that implementation remains the central focus for leaders. Using research at every step of the improvement process should become part of the culture of the system.

The leaders continue to analyze and summarize information collected through the monitoring process in order to make informed decisions about next steps and future planning. They examine the evidence of implementation and impact as specified in their improvement plans. They also discuss what they have observed or heard while informally monitoring implementation of individual strategies. These data provide extremely useful feedback concerning the extent to which strategies are being carried out, whether they are having the desired outcomes, and whether unanticipated issues have emerged.

As district and school leaders review their data, they reflect on how their findings may affect their improvement plans. If this examination reveals that strategies are not being carried out as intended or they are not moving the district and schools toward the ideal state, then the teams consider revising their plans or timelines. Unanticipated issues that need to be addressed are included in the updated plans. Revisions may include replacing existing strategies; adding or deleting action steps; or adjusting the timeline, responsibilities, resources, or evidence of implementation or impact.

Changes to the district improvement plan are then communicated to the participating schools because these changes may necessitate adjustments to the campus improvement plans. Any significant changes to district and campus plans are communicated throughout the system.

6

Phase V

Assessing and Reflecting on Outcomes

Assessing and Reflecting on Outcomes is the fifth of the five phases involved in the systemic improvement approach. Although leaders will have evaluated and reflected on the improvement work in previous phases, in Phase V, they consider the overall effectiveness of their planned strategies and actions based on summative year-end student performance and other impact data. The evaluation and reflection in this final phase become much more summative in nature.

Although this is the last of the five phases in the systemic approach, it does not represent an end to the improvement work because the process is cyclical in nature. In Phase V, leaders determine the focus for continuing the work. It is also a time for an important—and sometimes neglected—element of the improvement process: celebration of accomplishments. Phase V consists or three steps:

1. Analyze and Reflect on Evidence of Implementation and Impact

2. Decide on a Focus for Continuing the Improvement Work

3. Recognize Work, Progress, and Accomplishments

ANALYZE AND REFLECT ON EVIDENCE OF IMPLEMENTATION AND IMPACT

In order to evaluate progress on a systemwide basis, the district leadership team needs information from each of the participating schools about their accomplishments and challenges in reaching their own and the district's ideal state. Because outcomes are typically framed in terms of increased student achievement, the leadership team initiates the review process as soon as year-end achievement results are available.

The district team directs each school leadership team to analyze data and prepare a summary report. A comparison of student achievement data in content areas before and after implementation of the improvement plan is included in this report. Implementation and impact data specified in the school improvement plan (including any revisions to the improvement plan) should also be a major focus of this report. Other sources of data may include

- the Rubric for Determining System Capacity (Appendix III);
- formal and informal assessments of student progress not included in the improvement plan;
- summaries of classroom walkthrough data;
- one or more sections of the System Examination Tool (Appendix I);
- meeting agendas and notes from school leadership team meetings; and
- the discussions, input, and decisions that took place over the course of the school year among school leadership team members and among school staff.

The report is not intended to evaluate whether or not the school "passed or failed." Rather, the purpose of this document is to provide a starting point for a conversation among school and district leaders about the progress of the system as a whole in reaching the ideal state.

Before examining these data, school leaders revisit federal, state, and local goals or requirements for student achievement and review how to interpret the various data reports. Working in small groups the team compares their student learning outcomes to these goals and requirements in order to identify successes and continuing challenges.

This process is repeated for each set of data. The team then looks across the data sets to find consistencies, inconsistencies, and other interesting information from their data. They reflect on their findings to identify continuing and or emerging systemic issues that need to be addressed in the ongoing improvement work.

Using the Summative Analysis and Reflection Guide (Table 2), the school leaders also provide an overall summary of the extent to which they implemented the work as planned and whether it had the desired impact. They support their findings with specific evidence and examples so that district leaders can see how conclusions were drawn. The report strikes a balance between highlighting successes and identifying challenges that the school will need to overcome as the work continues.

Table 2   Summative Analysis and Reflection Guide

Implementation

1. In this current school year, to what extent have staff members effectively carried out their assignments related to the improvement effort as planned?

2. In what ways have leaders effectively monitored the work done and provided timely direction and support to the staff members carrying out the improvement work at all levels of the system?

3. What challenges or difficulties did leaders and teachers encounter while implementing the improvement plan and monitoring implementation?

4. What successes or accomplishments did staff members experience while implementing the improvement plan and monitoring implementation?

5. What are the insights that leaders have gained this year about implementing and monitoring the improvement plan, and how can they be used when planning for the coming year?

Impact

6. How has the implementation of the improvement plan achieved the intended outcomes as defined by the campus leadership team in the plan?

7. What changes in student achievement scores have occurred since the beginning of the improvement work?

8. What changes have occurred in the daily work at the district, school, and classroom levels that support the alignment of curriculum, instruction, and assessment to the state standards?

The district team replicates the process used at the school level for analyzing data, including revisiting federal, state, and local goals for student achievement and identifying trends and other information revealed by various data sets. The team begins its formal assessment and reflection by determining to what degree the district and school improvement plans have been implemented and monitored as intended. Team members compare student achievement data in the content areas before and after implementation of the improvement plan at each of the schools. They also compare the achievement level of each participating school to other schools in the district and to overall district results. They also review similar sources of data examined by the school team (e.g., the Rubric for Determining System Capacity, formal and informal assessments of student progress, survey data, etc.).

Implementation and impact data specified in the district improvement plan (including any revisions) are a major focus of this analysis. Summative results reveal how the overall system is progressing and whether the current effort is on track for achieving the ultimate goal of increasing student achievement. The analysis also has implications for the future direction of the work. This progress review focuses on the following questions:

1. Did the district and schools do what they set out to do? (Implementation)

2. Did the actions taken at the district and school levels make a difference in teaching and learning? (Impact)

Members of the district leadership team collaboratively analyze and reflect on the progress and challenges encountered at both the district and school levels, citing specific evidence and examples to support conclusions. This analysis helps identify key issues and sets the stage for discussions about the starting point and direction of the work in the coming year. It can also be used to communicate progress and future plans to internal and external stakeholders.

DECIDE ON A FOCUS FOR CONTINUING THE IMPROVEMENT WORK

The next steps for continuing the work in the coming year are determined by district and school issues that emerge from the summative analysis and reflection process. District leadership team members review the progress that has been made to date and consider the extent to which identified problems were addressed in the past year's plan. They should keep in mind that large-scale systemic change is often incremental and student achievement gains may not occur in the first year of implementation as new processes are introduced and capacity is built.

For issues that *were* addressed in the plan, the team members determine whether there were any substantial problems with *implementation* of the relevant strategies. They also identify which specific *action steps*, if implemented, were effective in carrying out the strategy.

If strategies or action steps *were not* carried out as intended, the team discusses why this happened and what should be done to ensure future implementation. They may decide to (1) establish a stronger commitment to the improvement work or (2) adjust the scope and/or timeline of the improvement plan so it can be accomplished. The discussion may reveal that a particular strategy or action step was not implemented for the simple reason that it was not appropriate or that resources were not available to support implementation.

If leaders decide to make considerable revisions to the scope of the existing improvement plan, they ensure that the work remains focused on achieving the *ideal state* as a means to increase student learning. The revised plan must remain substantial enough to have a significant impact on achieving this goal.

If leaders determine that the improvement plan *was* implemented and monitored effectively, they analyze whether the strategies had their intended results. If the desired impact was achieved, the team considers how to ensure sustainability of these strategies within the improved system, as well as how to recognize success.

However, if the intended impact was *not* realized, leaders may determine that the strategies or resources were inadequate for achieving intended outcomes. This finding requires leaders to examine the research and reconsider their strategies and available resources. Additional or more effective strategies may need to be included in the revised improvement plan for the coming year. Leaders follow a similar procedure in determining how effective the objectives were in reaching the ideal state or goal.

It is quite likely that a similar analysis at the school level will reveal that some schools in the system may need more time and assistance to achieve their goals and objectives. In such instances, the district determines additional support and pressure, if necessary, required by those schools.

At the same time, other schools that have had successful results may be ready to move forward, and the district must support these schools in their continued improvement efforts as well. The decision of whether to expand or intensify the current work or to shift the focus area (e.g., from curriculum to instruction) is based on the needs of schools in both of the situations described earlier.

When team members agree that their current focus area is successful and sustainable, they consider expanding the work by shifting to a new focus area, as described previously, or moving to a new content area (e.g., from mathematics to reading). This usually occurs as leaders and staff become comfortable with the approach, observe its positive impact firsthand, and gain more experience coordinating their efforts. In either case, they cycle back to the specific point in the systemic process that is most appropriate for beginning the work in the next school year.

The team cannot assume, however, that once they have achieved desired outcomes in a certain area, it no longer requires attention. Areas of success need ongoing monitoring and support to ensure that effective strategies remain standard ways of working and to maintain momentum for continuous improvement.

At this point, the district leadership team outlines a strategy for communicating their decisions regarding continuation of the systemic work to school leaders, the school board, the local community, and parents. District team members ensure that stakeholders have a clear understanding of progress made, challenges that remain, and the district focus for the coming year. Sharing information of this nature fosters ongoing support for cohesive and coherent improvement efforts and strengthens relationships that have been established both within and outside the school and district.

Representatives from the district team help school leaders understand the implications of the revised district plan for the school and classroom levels in order to refine their school improvement plans accordingly. They assist the school teams in determining next steps for their improvement work. The data on implementation and impact at the school level informs decisions on whether to revise the existing strategies, expand current efforts, or focus on a new content area in the school plan. In any case, the revised school improvement plan should remain aligned to the district plan, and the two plans should continue to be mutually supportive.

RECOGNIZE WORK, PROGRESS, AND ACCOMPLISHMENTS

Taking time to recognize the efforts and achievements of teachers and leaders is an important aspect of promoting long-term success in systemic improvement. Staff members develop a greater sense of ownership and are more likely to support the overall effort when they are acknowledged for their contributions and see real progress toward improving student achievement as a result of their work.

Leadership teams should make a conscious effort to identify and celebrate the contributions made by staff members at all levels of the system. Leaders at the district and school levels summarize accomplishments and progress made to date. The leaders then clearly articulate how each accomplishment advances the system toward its ideal state.

The informal recognition of staff involvement is an integral part of the monitoring that occurs throughout the improvement work. However, at this point, leaders recognize more formally the contributions of staff as a whole in reaching identified goals and objectives.

Once leaders identify district- and school-level accomplishments, they determine the specific strategies they will use to recognize staff members for their contributions. The precise nature of this recognition may vary from school to school, and leaders at each school must identify what type of recognition is most meaningful for their staff. For example, in one school, an informal celebration, such as an ice cream social, may be appropriate. In another school, a more formal recognition of the principal and teacher leaders at a faculty meeting or at a school board meeting may work best. Understanding the district and school cultures helps leaders make the best decisions for recognizing accomplishments.

Getting Serious About the System

What It Takes

This book is intended to describe the basic components and processes for a systemic improvement approach. The approach is not another quick fix that addresses only a single aspect of the educational system. Rather, it provides a process for examining trends and patterns, systemic structures, and mental models operating within a system that promote or inhibit continuous improvement.

In working with its partner sites, SEDL found that using the Working Systemically approach required that the local educational system demonstrate the following:

- A long-term commitment by leaders at the school and district levels to be actively engaged in the improvement process
- An initial focus on ensuring alignment of curriculum, instruction, and assessment to common core or state standards
- A commitment to collecting, interpreting, and using data to develop and monitor the improvement plan
- A sense of ownership and responsibility for improvement by staff members at all levels of the system

Reform of this nature also requires skilled leadership to help create a context for change, develop necessary knowledge and competencies, and establish structures and practices to support and maintain improvement. These leaders help district and school staff identify weaknesses in their system and guide them toward research-based, content-specific strategies to improve.

Therefore, the effort required to implement systemic improvement should not be underestimated. Adopting new and more effective research-based practices often requires changing long-established habits and patterns. Sharing leadership and creating a culture that values collaboration, continuous learning, and professional respect and trust call for significant changes in organizational structures and relationships among district and school staff.

The more detailed *Getting Serious About the System: A Fieldbook for District and School Leaders* provides in-depth information on how to implement a systemic improvement approach in district and schools. In addition to a detailed description of each phase and step of the systemic process, it provides access to online modules that include facilitator guides, PowerPoint slides, and handouts that will be useful to district and school leaders who will be guiding the improvement process.

Appendix I

System Examination Tool—Standards

This tool is designed to help members of the leadership team compare conditions and practices in their system to those in high-performing districts and schools. The tool is divided into the eight components of systemic improvement, with one page dedicated to each component.

Instructions:

- Examine the indicators on the left—what high-performing districts/ schools do.
- Underline those elements that are *well* supported by the local system and circle those elements that are *not* well supported by the system.
- Use collected data to describe the level of support provided. In the space provided, cite specific examples, where possible, for evidence of how the local system compares.

Indicators From High-Performing Districts/Schools	Evidence of How Our System Compares
• State standards are explicitly used to align the content-area curriculum and assessments that are used for instruction.	
• There is a clear expectation that all students will be proficient in the content areas outlined in the state standards.	
• Ongoing, job-embedded professional development is provided so all educators understand the content-area standards and are able to use the standards to guide their work.	
• Frequent follow-up and monitoring is provided to ensure that content-area instruction is focused on helping every student achieve the goals and benchmarks outlined in the state standards.	

System Examination Tool—Curriculum

This tool is designed to help members of the leadership team compare conditions and practices in their system to those in high-performing districts and schools. The tool is divided into the eight components of systemic improvement, with one page dedicated to each component.

Instructions:

- Examine the indicators on the left—what high-performing districts/schools do.
- Underline those elements that are *well* supported by the local system and circle those elements that are *not* well supported by the system.
- Use collected data to describe the level of support provided. In the space provided, cite specific examples, where possible, for evidence of how the local system compares.

Indicators From High-Performing Districts/Schools	*Evidence of How Our System Compares*
• Content-area instruction is clearly aligned with the standards, curriculum, and assessments. • Content-area instruction is designed to ensure that students are engaged in meaningful instructional activities. • All teachers demonstrate high expectations for every student to perform proficiently. • All teachers take personal responsibility for helping every student achieve his or her full potential. • Teachers tailor instruction to meet the individual needs of diverse learners.	

System Examination Tool—Instruction

This tool is designed to help members of the leadership team compare conditions and practices in their system to those in high-performing districts and schools. The tool is divided into the eight components of systemic improvement, with one page dedicated to each component.

Instructions:

- Examine the indicators on the left—what high-performing districts/schools do.
- Underline those elements that are *well* supported by the local system and circle those elements that are *not* well supported by the system.
- Use collected data to describe the level of support provided. In the space provided, cite specific examples, where possible, for evidence of how the local system compares.

Indicators From High-Performing Districts/Schools	Evidence of How Our System Compares
• Content-area instruction is clearly aligned with the standards, curriculum, and assessments.	
• Content-area instruction is designed to ensure that students are engaged in meaningful instructional activities.	
• All teachers demonstrate high expectations for every student to perform proficiently.	
• All teachers take personal responsibility for helping every student achieve his or her full potential.	
• Teachers tailor instruction to meet the individual needs of diverse learners.	
• Teachers participate in ongoing professional development activities that enable them to provide high-quality content-area instruction that supports student needs.	
• Classroom instruction is frequently monitored to ensure teachers are providing high-quality content-area instruction that supports student needs.	

System Examination Tool—Assessment

This tool is designed to help members of the leadership team compare conditions and practices in their system to those in high-performing districts and schools. The tool is divided into the eight components of systemic improvement, with one page dedicated to each component.

Instructions:

- Examine the indicators on the left—what high-performing districts/ schools do.
- Underline those elements that are *well* supported by the local system and circle those elements that are *not* well supported by the system.
- Use collected data to describe the level of support provided. In the space provided, cite specific examples, where possible, for evidence of how the local system compares.

Indicators From High-Performing Districts/Schools	*Evidence of How Our System Compares*
• All content-area assessments are clearly aligned with the curriculum, instruction, and state standards.	
• All educators understand and are able to interpret content-area assessment data.	
• A variety of formal and informal assessments are used regularly to monitor students' progress and to identify individual student learning needs.	
• Teachers collaboratively study student data and decide on appropriate adjustments to lessons.	
• Data from content-area assessments are organized and arrayed in a user-friendly format, then shared in a timely manner with all stakeholders, including parents.	
• High-quality professional development is provided to ensure that all staff understand the content-area assessments and know how to interpret and use assessment data to guide instruction.	
• Classrooms are monitored to ensure that teachers are using assessment data to inform content-area instruction.	

System Examination Tool—Resources

This tool is designed to help members of the leadership team compare conditions and practices in their system to those in high-performing districts and schools. The tool is divided into the eight components of systemic improvement, with one page dedicated to each component.

Instructions:

- Examine the indicators on the left—what high-performing districts/ schools do.
- Underline those elements that are *well* supported by the local system and circle those elements that are *not* well supported by the system.
- Use collected data to describe the level of support provided. In the space provided, cite specific examples, where possible, for evidence of how the local system compares.

Indicators From High-Performing Districts/Schools	Evidence of How Our System Compares
• The materials available for content-area instruction are aligned with and clearly support the district's curriculum and state standards.	
• Materials used for content-area instruction are high quality and their use is supported by research.	
• Teachers ensure there is adequate time for uninterrupted instruction in the content area.	
• Time is provided for regular collaborative meetings among teachers and administrators to discuss content-area instructional issues.	
• A content-area curriculum leader is available to provide instructional support for teachers.	
• Teachers regularly participate in professional development activities that support effective content-area instruction and affect student achievement.	
• Instruction in the content area and professional development activities are monitored to ensure that time and resources are used as effectively as possible.	

System Examination Tool— Professional Staff

This tool is designed to help members of the leadership team compare conditions and practices in their system to those in high-performing districts and schools. The tool is divided into the eight components of systemic improvement, with one page dedicated to each component.

Instructions:

- Examine the indicators on the left—what high-performing districts/ schools do.
- Underline those elements that are *well* supported by the local system and circle those elements that are *not* well supported by the system.
- Use collected data to describe the level of support provided. In the space provided, cite specific examples, where possible, for evidence of how the local system compares.

Indicators From High-Performing Districts/Schools	Evidence of How Our System Compares
• The district/school provides job-embedded, ongoing professional development for everyone at all levels.	
• The district/school uses data proactively to recruit, select, train, and place effective teachers and leaders.	
• The district/school has an accountability system that monitors staff effectiveness.	
• The district/school has a system for rewarding/recognizing teachers and leaders who produce desired learner outcomes.	
• The district/school communicates expectations for a supportive organizational culture built on trust, respect, and collaboration.	
• The district/school utilizes internal and external experts to provide mentoring, coaching, and other support to individual leaders and teachers.	

System Examination Tool—
Policy and Governance

This tool is designed to help members of the leadership team compare conditions and practices in their system to those in high-performing districts and schools. The tool is divided into the eight components of systemic improvement, with one page dedicated to each component.

Instructions:

- Examine the indicators on the left—what high-performing districts/schools do.
- Underline those elements that are *well* supported by the local system and circle those elements that are *not* well supported by the system.
- Use collected data to describe the level of support provided. In the space provided, cite specific examples, where possible, for evidence of how the local system compares.

Indicators From High-Performing Districts/Schools	Evidence of How Our System Compares
• The district/school has a multimeasure accountability system and uses data systemwide to inform practice, to monitor progress, and to hold district and school leaders accountable for results.	
• The district/school monitors its actions and decisions to ensure that they contribute to their long-range vision.	
• The district's/school's policy and governance convey a strong belief in the capacity of school system personnel to maintain high standards of learning for all students and high standards of teaching and leadership from all instructional and support staff.	
• The district/school establishes non-negotiable goals for instruction and achievement through a collaborative process.	
• The district/school enacts policy that ensures equitable opportunities and outcomes for students through purposeful distribution of resources (i.e., time, money, personnel).	
• The district/school establishes organizational structures, roles, and responsibilities to support the vision for improvement.	

System Examination Tool—
Family and Community

This tool is designed to help members of the leadership team compare conditions and practices in their system to those in high-performing districts and schools. The tool is divided into the eight components of systemic improvement, with one page dedicated to each component.

Instructions:

- Examine the indicators on the left—what high-performing districts/schools do.
- Underline those elements that are *well* supported by the local system and circle those elements that are *not* well supported by the system.
- Use collected data to describe the level of support provided. In the space provided, cite specific examples, where possible, for evidence of how the local system compares.

Indicators From High-Performing Districts/Schools	*Evidence of How Our System Compares*
• The district/school instills visions that focus on student learning and guide instructional improvement involving families and communities.	
• The district/school assesses community values and interests and translates these into a vision for improvement.	
• The district/school builds relationships with the community based on respect, trust, confidence, support, and open communication.	
• The district/school builds commitment to improvement goals among parents and community.	
• The district/school promotes and coordinates stakeholders' involvement in improvement efforts and builds capacity as needed.	
• The district/school promotes effective two-way communication between the school system and the public.	
• The district/school uses data to assess and refine their family and community engagement efforts.	

Appendix II

Leadership Self-Assessment

Communicating Clear Expectations

Leaders keep the goals of the improvement effort a priority at all levels of the local system.

A. Leaders communicate clearly that the activities specified in the improvement plans are, and will remain, a priority.

Ideal				Unacceptable
①	②	③	④	⑤
Leaders consistently refer to the improvement plans in school documents, meeting agendas, and daily interactions to ensure that all staff understand the expectation to implement the action steps in the plans so that all students will become proficient in state standards.	Leaders often refer to the improvement plans in school documents, meeting agendas, and daily interactions to communicate that staff are expected to implement the action steps in the plans so that all students will become proficient in state standards.	Leaders occasionally review the improvement plans at staff meetings and announce early in the year that staff are expected to work on the actions steps so that students will become proficient in state standards.	Leaders give the staff the improvement plans and communicate to staff that they should implement the action steps.	Leaders do not disseminate the improvement plans, and staff are unaware of goals, objectives, strategies, and action steps included in the plans.
①	②	③	④	
Leaders ensure that necessary time and other resources are available to support implementation of the action steps in the improvement plans so that all students will become proficient in state standards.	Leaders provide time and some other resources to support implementation of the action steps in the improvement plans.	Leaders provide limited time and few other resources to implement the action steps in the improvement plans.	Leaders provide no time or other resources to implement the action steps in the improvement plans.	

Communicating Clear Expectations

Leaders keep the goals of the improvement effort a priority at all levels of the local system.

B. *Leaders keep the work of the improvement effort continuous.*

Ideal				Unacceptable
①	②	③	④	⑤
Leaders schedule and attend regular meetings with small groups of staff to engage in professional conversations that will assist them in understanding their roles and tasks in the district and school plans for improving student achievement.	Leaders engage staff at monthly all-staff meetings in professional conversations about their assigned tasks in the district and school plans for improving student achievement.	Leaders provide structures (e.g., time at staff meetings) for staff to converse with others about their assigned tasks in the district and school plans for improving student achievement.	Leaders seldom discuss the district and school plans with staff after the plans are distributed.	
①	②	③	④	⑤
Leaders regularly and personally communicate with each staff member to emphasize the importance of implementing the district and school plans for improving student achievement.	Leaders communicate personally a few times with each staff member to emphasize the importance of implementing the district and school plans for improving student achievement.	Leaders occasionally communicate personally with some staff members to emphasize the importance of implementing the district and school plans for improving student achievement.	Leaders seldom communicate with individual staff members about the district and school improvement plans.	Leaders do not mention the district and school improvement plans after they are introduced in their interactions with staff members.

(Continued)

Communicating Clear Expectations

Leaders keep the goals of the improvement effort a priority at all levels of the local system.

C. *Leaders keep the improvement work the central focus for the district and school leadership teams.*

Ideal			Unacceptable	
①	②	③	④	⑤
Leaders focus every meeting of the leadership teams on implementation and impact of the improvement plans.	Leaders focus most meetings of the leadership teams on implementation and impact of the improvement plans.	Leaders focus some meetings of the leadership teams on implementation and impact of the improvement plans.	Leaders focus some meetings of the leadership teams on implementation of the improvement plans, but seldom look at impact.	Leaders do not focus on the implementation or impact of the improvement plans at leadership team meetings.
①	②	③	④	⑤
Leaders consistently embed learning opportunities that support specific district and school goals into regularly scheduled meetings of administrators and teachers. They frequently facilitate follow-up conversations about how the learning applies to district and school improvement.	Leaders often embed learning opportunities that support specific district and school goals into regularly scheduled meetings of administrators and teachers. They sometimes facilitate follow-up conversations about how the learning applies to district and school improvement.	Leaders sometimes embed learning opportunities that support general district and school goals into scheduled meetings of administrators and teachers. They rarely facilitate follow-up conversations about how the learning applies to district and school improvement.	Leaders rarely embed learning opportunities into scheduled meetings of administrators and teachers. They do not make connections between the learning and district and school improvement.	Leaders do not embed learning opportunities into scheduled meetings of administrators and teachers.

①	②	③	④	
Leaders regularly and frequently communicate with each other to maintain a focus on the improvement effort.	Leaders sometimes communicate with each other about the focus of the improvement effort.	Leaders communicate with each other on a variety of issues, often unrelated to the improvement effort.	Leaders rarely communicate with each other about the improvement effort outside of scheduled meetings.	

(Continued)

65

Building Capacity

Leaders ensure that staff members have what they need in order to succeed in the necessary tasks.

A. Leaders ensure that staff members develop and apply needed knowledge and skills to carry out the improvement work successfully.

Ideal			Unacceptable	
①	②	③	④	⑤
Leaders ensure that a professional development plan for teachers and administrators is in place before the school year begins. Professional development is based on data and input from the schools, is ongoing and job-embedded, incorporates specific follow-up, and includes adequate time and other resources.	Leaders provide a professional development plan for teachers and administrators soon after the school year begins. Professional development is ongoing and job-embedded, incorporates specific follow-up, and includes adequate time and other resources.	Leaders provide a professional development plan for teachers sometime after the school year begins. Professional development is ongoing and job-embedded, incorporates specific follow-up, and includes adequate time and other resources.	Leaders provide a professional development plan for teachers that specifies the content for workshops, but includes only limited follow-up, time, or other resources.	Leaders schedule professional development days on the district and school calendars with no specific plan for the content or scope of the professional development.
①	②	③	④	
Leaders ensure that teachers engage in meaningful long-term professional development. They provide for ongoing instructional support and follow-up to ensure that new knowledge and skills are put into practice.	Leaders ensure that teachers engage in meaningful professional development. They provide for some instructional support and follow-up to ensure that new knowledge and skills are put into practice.	Leaders ensure that teachers engage in professional development but provide little ongoing instructional support and follow-up to ensure that new knowledge and skills are put into practice.	Leaders allow teachers to make individual choices about their professional development and provide little, if any, follow-up support to ensure that new knowledge and skills are put into practice.	

Building Capacity

Leaders ensure that staff members have what they need in order to succeed in the necessary tasks.

B. *Leaders ensure that the required resources, including time and staff, are available to meet the identified needs of the system.*

Ideal				Unacceptable
①	②	③	④	⑤
Leaders provide standards-based curriculum materials (including a scope and sequence), data summaries, research summaries, and all necessary resources to support school-level collaboration to address the needs of the system.	Leaders provide standards-based curriculum materials (including a scope and sequence) and some other resources to support school-level collaboration to address the needs of the system.	Leaders provide curriculum materials and some other resources to support collaboration among content specialists in addressing the needs of the system.	Leaders provide limited resources for collaboration to address the needs of the system.	Leaders do not provide resources for collaboration to address the needs of the system.
①	②	③	④	⑤
Leaders allocate regularly scheduled time each week during the school day for teachers to collaborate on aligning their instruction and assessment to state standards and the district curriculum.	Leaders allocate regularly scheduled time twice each month during the school day for teachers to collaborate on aligning their instruction and assessment to state standards and the district curriculum.	Leaders provide occasional opportunities for teachers to collaborate on aligning their instruction and assessment to state standards and the district curriculum.	Leaders encourage teachers to work in groups to plan special events or discuss school projects related to the instructional program.	Leaders make no provisions for teachers to work together on school events or projects related to the instructional program.

(Continued)

Building Capacity (Continued)

①	②	③	④
Leaders regularly and frequently solicit input from staff regarding needs for a variety of instructional resources aligned to state standards, the district curriculum, and specific student learning needs.	Leaders often solicit input from staff regarding needs for instructional resources aligned to state standards, the district curriculum, and general student learning needs.	Leaders occasionally solicit input from staff regarding needs for instructional resources. There is no overt alignment of these resources to state standards, the district curriculum, or student learning needs.	Leaders rarely, if ever, solicit input from staff regarding needs for instructional resources. They make little or no attempt to align such resources to standards or student needs.

Monitoring and Reviewing
Leaders monitor implementation and impact of the planned work.

A. Leaders design a system to monitor implementation of the improvement plans and their impact on student achievement.

Ideal				Unacceptable
①	②	③	④	⑤
Leaders ensure that a system is in place to collect and analyze data from multiple sources relevant to the quality of the instructional program in the district and schools. They monitor implementation and impact data for all action steps in improvement plans and discuss their findings with leadership teams and staff at all levels of the system at least every two months.	Leaders ensure that a system is in place to collect and analyze data from multiple sources relevant to the quality of the instructional program in the district and schools. They monitor implementation and impact data for most action steps in improvement plans and discuss their findings with leadership teams three to four times every year.	Leaders collect and analyze limited data from a few sources relevant to the quality of the instructional program in the district and schools. They monitor implementation and impact data for selected action steps in improvement plans and discuss their findings with key staff two times a year.	Leaders collect data from only one or two sources relevant to the quality of the instructional program in the district and schools. They monitor data implementation only for selected action steps in improvement plans and discuss their findings among themselves.	Leaders collect no data relevant to the quality of the instructional program and do not monitor implementation of action steps in their improvement plans.

(Continued)

69

Monitoring and Reviewing (Continued)

①	②	③	④	⑤
Leaders use disaggregated data from multiple sources (including annual and benchmark assessment) to monitor student performance at least four times a year. They provide assistance to help the leadership team and the staff interpret and act on the results.	Leaders use disaggregated data only from annual and benchmark assessments to monitor student performance two times a year. They provide assistance to help the leadership team and the staff interpret and act on the results.	Leaders use results of annual and benchmark assessments to monitor student performance. They work with the leadership team to interpret and act on the results.	Leaders review the state-mandated test results at the end of each year to determine student progress but have no plan for assisting staff in interpreting or acting on the results.	Leaders review the state-mandated test results at the end of each year only to determine the district and school status in the accountability system.

Monitoring and Reviewing

Leaders monitor implementation and impact of the planned work.

B. *Leaders confer on a regular basis with individuals carrying out the improvement plans and work proactively to address issues that arise.*

Ideal				Unacceptable
①	②	③	④	⑤
Leaders meet monthly with staff at all levels of the system, both as a group and individually, as needed, to review progress in carrying out the improvement plans. They agree on specific interventions and assistance to staff and students who do not demonstrate proficiency in the skills required to achieve anticipated results.	Leaders meet three to four times a year with staff at all levels of the system as a group to review progress in carrying out the improvement plans. They discuss general interventions and assistance for staff and students who do not demonstrate proficiency in skills required to achieve anticipated results.	Leaders meet twice a year with staff at all levels of the system to review progress in carrying out the improvement plans. They focus primarily on interventions that may be used with students who are not achieving desired results.	Leaders meet with staff at the end of the year to discuss progress in carrying out the improvement plans. They discuss changes in the improvement plans for the next year.	Leaders do not meet with staff to discuss progress in carrying out the improvement plans at the end of the year.

Appendix II

Rubric for Determining System Capacity

This is a tool that may be used to help determine the capacity of the education system. Look at each question and the subsequent statements to decide whether the system is a "3," a "2," or a "1" (use decimals if the rating is somewhere in between two categories). In the space provided, indicate the source of data used for making that judgment. The ratings can be an aid in prioritizing the system's needs.

Determining System Capacity

School District _____   Date _____

Questions	What it looks like			Evidence of current status and any progress
	3	2	1	
	Creating Coherence			
Does the system have a curriculum that is aligned to state standards?	Curriculum is clearly aligned to state standards.	A district curriculum is in place but is out-of-date and not aligned to current state standards.	Teachers use their textbook as a curriculum.	
Does the system ensure that the selection of programs and use of resources are aligned to the curriculum?	Programs are selected on how well they support the district curriculum. Resources are allocated to support the district curriculum.	Programs are aligned to the district curriculum, but there is no clear connection among them. Resources are distributed by formula.	Many disconnected programs and initiatives are in place. Resources are distributed to programs that get the most notice.	
Does the system have a curriculum scope and sequence that identifies what students should know and be able to do at each grade level?	District curriculum includes a scope and sequence. Curriculum specifies knowledge and skill by grade level.	District curriculum is in place and available. No scope and sequence exists. Student learning expectations are more general than specific.	Teachers determine learning expectations for their own students.	

Does the system create clear expectations that teachers use a curriculum aligned to state standards to guide their instruction?		Teachers can describe how they use their curriculum to guide instruction.	Teachers are aware of the district curriculum, but there is little evidence that it is used to guide instruction.	Teachers' instruction has no clear connection to curriculum or state standards.
Does the system ensure that content expertise is available and utilized appropriately so that research-based strategies are used in the classroom?		Timely content support is available for teachers on-site from either the school or district level or external sources.	Individuals have been given the role of content support specialists at the district or school level but have limited interaction with teachers.	No formal content support is available at the school or district level.

Determining System Capacity

Questions	What it looks like			Evidence of current status and any progress
	3	2	1	
Does the system have a process for collecting and organizing disaggregated student-learning data in an understandable and useful format?	Student mastery of the standards is regularly monitored. The district generates disaggregated trend data on student achievement and analyzes it with school leaders at least twice every year.	Student mastery of the standards is measured more than once per year. The district generates disaggregated trend data on student achievement and shares them with schools annually.	Student mastery of the standards is only measured by annual standardized tests. Student achievement results generated by the state or a publisher are distributed to the schools.	
Does the system use multiple types of data (student learning, school processes, demographics, and perceptions) to get to a better understanding of problems and to formulate plans?	The district examines the relationship between multiple types of data and looks for underlying causes of poor academic progress to develop improvement plans.	The district uses more than annual student achievement data and looks for underlying causes of poor academic progress to develop improvement plans.	The district and school use only annual student achievement data to develop improvement plans.	
Does the system use data from informal classroom observations to monitor instruction?	Informal classroom walkthroughs are conducted regularly, and regular feedback is provided.	Classrooms are visited regularly for formal observation used for teacher evaluation and feedback is tied to evaluations.	Classrooms are rarely visited, if ever, and teachers do not get feedback on their instruction.	

Does the system have processes for turning data into action that provides timely interventions for students who are not mastering the standards?	The district, schools, and teachers use frequent formative assessment to track student progress and provide immediate interventions for students before they fall behind.	The schools provide tutoring throughout the year for students whose grades are falling behind and summer school for students who have failed.	The schools provide summer school for students who have failed.

Determining System Capacity

Ensuring Continuous Professional Learning

Questions	What it looks like			Evidence of current status and any progress
	3	2	1	
Does the system ensure that professional learning opportunities are data driven?	District and schools use student achievement data and data from monitoring classroom instruction, as well as survey data, to plan professional development.	District uses only annual student achievement data to plan all professional development.	Professional development plans are based on the personal priorities of district and school leaders or teachers' personal preferences.	
Does the system ensure that all professional learning opportunities are research based?	Teams that make decisions about creating professional learning opportunities have access to and *use* research that links an approach to improved student achievement.	Teams that make decisions about creating professional learning opportunities have access to research that links an approach to improved student achievement.	The system bases decisions about professional learning opportunities on personal opinion.	
Does the system set clear expectations for ways to improve professional practice at all levels of the system (classroom, school, and district)?	Teachers, principals, and central office members are all members of learning teams at the school and/or district level. Learning teams are supported and held accountable for improving professional practice.	Teachers are all members of small learning teams. Administrators support teachers by providing resources (time, money, and human resources) but do not monitor the work they do.	Teachers are expected to find or create their own professional development opportunities. Expectations for professional learning are in district and school policy, which is sporadically enforced.	

Does the system monitor the implementation of new strategies and practices and provide both pressure and support (coaching)?	All educators are expected to implement new strategies and practices. Leaders make frequent classroom visits, and support is readily available for teachers.	Expectations for implementing professional development exist but are vague. Support is available but sporadic.	Implementation of new strategies and practices is not monitored. Support is provided when requested.
Does the system provide adequate time for professional learning that is job embedded and promotes collaboration and active participation?	District policy provides time flexibility so there is time available for teachers during the day. Principals create time for collaboration on instructional issues during the school day.	The district provides some staff development days and early release days throughout the year. Staff development sessions actively engage individual participants.	The district provides some staff development days during the school year. Staff development consists of presentations to teachers.

Determining System Capacity

Questions	What it looks like			Evidence of current status and any progress
	Building Relationships			
	3	2	1	
Does the system provide multiple structures (including time) for individuals at different levels (district, school, classroom) to have professional conversations?	Collaborative teams at schools address specific instructional issues as part of their regular workday in a way that does not disrupt instruction. District-level teams, which include school-level staff, meet regularly to address instructional issues.	School-level teams focus on both instructional and administrative issues and are scheduled after school or in the evening. District-level teams deal with day-to-day issues and reflect on systemwide instructional issues	School-level teams are present but meetings are irregular and have no clear focus. District teams focus almost exclusively on administrative issues.	
Do the leaders encourage positive interactions among schools—both vertically and horizontally?	Feeder patterns of schools meet at least annually to focus on aligning instruction to meet the needs of students at all levels. Schools meet at least annually by level to focus on aligning instruction to meet the needs of students at all levels.	Feeder patterns of schools have met within the last two years to focus on aligning instruction to meet the needs of students at all levels. Schools have met by level within the last two years to focus on aligning instruction to meet the needs of students at all levels.	Schools within the district operate independently and have very little contact with one another.	

Does the system encourage positive interactions between the district and the schools?	District-level teams listen to the concerns of teachers and schools, solicit input on instructional needs, and generate solutions.	District-level teams solicit input from schools on mainly administrative matters.	District-level teams operate independently of any connection with the schools.
Does the system encourage positive interactions between the district and the community?	Both large and small public forums, focus groups, and informal meetings invite and respect multiple perspectives.	One or two large public forums are held during which the public is invited to speak.	Public meetings are the only forums for information sharing.

Determining System Capacity

Questions	Responding to Changing Conditions			Evidence of current status and any progress
	What it looks like			
	3	2	1	
Does the system have a process for anticipating and recognizing changing conditions that affect multiple levels of the local system?	School and district leaders track local, state, and national policy decisions for how they will affect the system. Demographic trends are closely monitored. The system has a leadership succession plan and follows it.	District leaders follow the state policy decisions. Demographic shifts trigger immediate action. Leadership changes equate to changes in practices and procedures.	The superintendent attends regional and state meetings and shares the information with the cabinet. The system is slow to respond to changes in demographics. Frequent leadership changes result in random changes in practices and procedures.	
Does the system promote and support innovations that help them adapt to changing conditions?	The system responds to changes by researching and selecting new approaches. The system fully supports those who take the risk of implementing new approaches.	The system is open to new ideas that are brought to them from external agencies. The system gives some support to those who take the risk of implementing new approaches.	New ideas and approaches are suspect. Innovations are tried but not fully supported or implemented.	

Does the system keep the focus on teaching and learning when conditions or circumstances change?	The system responds to the changes faced by thoroughly analyzing the implications of the change for teaching and learning. Approaches to address the changes are integrated with current priorities that focus on teaching and learning.	The system looks to see how other systems are addressing similar issues as it addresses teaching and learning. The system reacts by creating a new initiative that is related to current priorities that focus on teaching and learning.	The system reacts to changing conditions without reflecting on the impact on teaching and learning. The system reacts by creating a new initiative without making connections to current initiatives that support student learning.
Does the system seek current and relevant "best practice" and research to address changing conditions?	The system continually exposes district- and school-level teams to current research related to district goals. The system provides guidance for district and school teams on how to use educational research.	The system occasionally provides district- and school-level teams with information about research related to district goals.	The system does not provide information about educational research to decision-making teams.

References

Bernhardt, V. L. (2004). *Data analysis for comprehensive schoolwide improvement* (2nd ed.). Larchmont, NY: Eye On Education.

Blum, R., & Landis, S. (1998). *Scaling up continuous improvement: A case description of Onward to Excellence in Mississippi.* Portland, OR: Northwest Regional Educational Laboratory.

Bossert, S. (1985, May). Effective elementary schools. In R. Kyle (Ed.), *Reaching for excellence: An effective schools sourcebook* (pp. 39–53). Washington, DC: U.S. Government Printing Office.

Bryk, A. S., & Schneider, B. L. (2002). *Trust in schools: A core resource for improvement.* New York, NY: Russell Sage Foundation.

Bryk, A. S., Sebring, P. B., Allensworth, E., Luppescu, S., & Easton, J. Q. (2010). *Organizing schools for improvement: Lessons from Chicago.* Chicago, IL: University Of Chicago Press.

Chenowith, K. (2007). *"It's being done": Academic success in unexpected schools.* Cambridge, MA: Harvard Education Press.

Cohen, M., & Ginsburg, A. (2001, January). *School improvement report: Executive order on actions for turning around low-performing schools.* Washington, DC: U.S. Department of Education.

Corallo, C., & McDonald, D. H. (2002, January). *What works with low-performing schools: A review of research.* Charleston, WV: AEL.

Cowan, D. F. (2006). Creating learning communities in low-performing sites: A systemic approach to alignment. *Journal of School Leadership, 16*(5), 596–610.

Cowan, D. F., Joyner, S., & Beckwith, S. (2008). *Working systemically in action: A guide for facilitators.* Austin, TX: SEDL.

Edmonds, R. (1979). Effective schools for the urban poor. *Educational Leadership, 37*(1), 15–23.

Hallinger, P., & Murphy, J. (1986). The social context of effective schools. *American Journal of Education, 94*(3), 328–355.

Holcomb, E. L. (2008). *Asking the right questions: Tools for collaboration and school change* (3rd ed.). Thousand Oaks, CA: Corwin.

Huie, S. B., Buttram, J. L., Deviney, F. P., Murphy, K. M., & Ramos, M. A. (2004). *Alignment in SEDL's Working Systemically model* (Research report). Austin, TX: SEDL.

Jenlink, P. M., Reigeluth, C. M., Carr, A. A., & Nelson, L. M. (1998). Guidelines for facilitating systemic change in school districts. *Systems Research and Behavioral Science, 15*(3), 217–233.

Lezotte, L. W., & Jacoby, B. C. (1992). *Sustainable school reform: The district context for school improvement.* Okemos, MI: Effective Schools Products.

Mid-continent Research for Education and Learning. (2003). *Sustaining school improvement* (Leadership Folio Series). Aurora, CO: Author.

Murphy, J., & Meyers, C. V. (2008). *Turning around failing schools.* Thousand Oaks, CA: Corwin.

Newmann, F. M., Smith, B., Allensworth, E., & Bryk, A. S. (2001, Winter). Instructional program coherence: What it is and why it should guide school improvement policy. *Educational Evaluation and Policy Analysis, 23*(4), 213–227.

Rorrer, A. K., Skrla, L., & Scheurich, J. J. (2008). Districts as institutional actors in educational reform. *Educational Administration Quarterly, 44*(3), 307–358.

Sashkin, M., & Egermeier, J. (1993). *School change models and processes: A review and synthesis of research and practice.* Washington, DC: U.S. Department of Education.

Senge, P., Cambron-McCabe, N., Lucas, T., Smith, B., Dutton, J., & Kleiner, A. (2000). *Schools that learn.* New York, NY: Doubleday.

Sparks, D. (2004). Focusing staff development on improving the learning for all students. In G. Cawelti (Ed.), *Handbook of research on improving student achievement* (3rd ed., pp. 245–255). Arlington, VA: Educational Research Service.

Stringfield, S. (1995). Attempts to enhance students' learning: A search for valid programs and highly reliable implementation techniques. *School Effectiveness and School Improvement, 6*(1), 67–96.

Teddlie, C., & Stringfield, S. (1993). *School matters: Lessons learned from a 10-year study of school effects.* New York, NY: Teachers College Press.

Thornton, B., Shepperson, T., & Canavero, S. (2007). A systems approach to school improvement: Program evaluation and organizational learning. *Education, 128*(1), 48–55.

www.ingramcontent.com/pod-product-compliance
Lightning Source LLC
Jackson TN
JSHW061923310126
97517JS00013B/130